D0409651

THE ASSAULT
ON TRUTH

THE ASSAULT
ON TRUTH ·

BORIS JOHNSON, DONALD TRUMP
AND THE EMERGENCE OF A NEW
MORAL BARBARISM

PETER OBORNE

**SIMON &
SCHUSTER**

London · New York · Sydney · Toronto · New Delhi

First published in Great Britain by Simon & Schuster UK Ltd, 2021

Copyright © Peter Oborne, 2021

The right of Peter Oborne to be identified as the author of this work has been asserted in accordance with the Copyright, Designs and Patents Act, 1988.

5 7 9 10 8 6 4

Simon & Schuster UK Ltd
1st Floor
222 Gray's Inn Road
London WC1X 8HB

www.simonandschuster.co.uk
www.simonandschuster.com.au
www.simonandschuster.co.in

Simon & Schuster Australia, Sydney
Simon & Schuster India, New Delhi

The author and publishers have made all reasonable efforts to contact copyright-holders for permission, and apologise for any omissions or errors in the form of credits given. Corrections may be made to future printings.

A CIP catalogue record for this book is available from the British Library

Hardback ISBN: 978-1-3985-0100-3
eBook ISBN: 978-1-3985-0101-0

Typeset in Bembo by M Rules
Printed in the UK by CPI Group (UK) Ltd, Croydon, CR0 4YY

MIX
Paper from
responsible sources
FSC
www.fsc.org
FSC® C020471

'Oh, what a tangled web we weave, when first we practise to deceive!'

Walter Scott

CONTENTS

Chapter One

AN INTRODUCTION TO POLITICAL LYING

'It is of paramount importance that Ministers give accurate and truthful information to Parliament, correcting any inadvertent error at the earliest opportunity. Ministers who knowingly mislead Parliament will be expected to offer their resignation to the Prime Minister.'

MINISTERIAL CODE

You're looking to hire a new member of staff. A candidate presents himself. He is charming, intelligent, amusing, well connected, with glowing references. But a check throws up uncomfortable facts. He was sacked from his first job after university for lying. He was sacked again, after a similar episode, later on in his career. Close inspection reveals that he has a history of

1

deception, misrepresentation, false statements and serial fabrication.

You'd probably be more likely to call the police than hire this individual. And yet, on 12 December 2019, the British people elected Boris Johnson as prime minister.

In the first two chapters of this book I explain how this happened. This involves two tasks. The first is simple. I will use a mass of irrefutable evidence to prove that Johnson (and regrettably his most senior advisers and ministers as well) habitually lie, fabricate and misrepresent the facts. Such a weight of material is also a burden. Publishing it all would make this book too long. So I won't expose every lie.

I will then examine Johnson's methodology of deception. This means presenting some of the most vivid, shocking and powerful examples.

The second task is more complicated, but also more interesting. What led the British people to put a liar into Downing Street? And what made the Conservative Party, which has played such a famous role in British history, install him as leader?

The superficial answer is that he was lucky in his opponents, first in the Conservative leadership election and even more so in the general election of 2019. But for a full answer we need to look beyond Westminster and electoral politics.

It's not long since Britain was famed for both public and private probity. Liars were shunned, in private and public life. Under Boris Johnson political deceit has become not just commonplace but automatic. His election as prime minister suggests that British people no longer care about the difference between fact and fiction, or truth and falsehood. What kind of a society have we become?

It's unimaginable that a compulsive liar such as Johnson could have been chosen to lead the Conservative Party in a previous era, let alone elected prime minister. There was a time, before the emergence of political parties as we know them today, when it was normal for ministers to lie, cheat and bribe. In the eighteenth century, many of Britain's most famous writers and journalists were paid by the government to apply their literary skills to undermine opponents. Meanwhile ministers made huge sums from corruption, vindicating Ambrose Bierce's famous description of politics as 'the conduct of public affairs for private advantage'.* Ministers did not want voters (or rival politicians) to know how government money was being spent. So there was limited accountability and often zero integrity in public administration.

In Chapter Three I will show how morality changed in public life. Our Victorian ancestors, many inspired by evangelical Christianity, erected a series of protections against deceit and corruption. It is fashionable to mock them today, but the Victorians brought high ideals into government which changed the way that Britain was ruled.

---

* Ambrose Bierce, *The Devil's Dictionary* (London: Arthur F. Bird, 1906), https://www.gutenberg.org/files/972/972-h/972-h.htm.

They introduced accountability and integrity, in the process creating the modern British state.

The Victorian system, based on the rule of law and an honest, impartial civil service, lasted throughout the twentieth century. It made the great majority of Britons believe in the basic good faith of their governments, and therefore to accept the sacrifices necessary to fight two world wars. During this century lying to Parliament, or being caught out lying to Parliament, was one of the most serious sins any British politician could commit.

Ministers, human nature being what it is, continued to lie and cheat. But their misdemeanours were individual, not structural. Once caught out they were shamed and their careers destroyed. That explains why in twentieth-century Britain, political deception was typically committed by rogue individuals acting without the knowledge (and against the doctrines) of the institutions they served.

The first serious threat to this system came with the election of New Labour in 1997. Tony Blair and his ministers made a logical (and in some ways understandable) error.

The left has a tendency to believe that it is uniquely virtuous, and that this special virtue gives it a privileged relationship with the truth. In particular left-wing movements feel that in a venal world filled with vicious, unscrupulous right-wing enemies they are licensed to use falsehood to secure their political ends. That was especially true in the 1930s, when left-wingers were understandably desperate to stop fascism and Nazism. They manufactured any kind of propaganda which might achieve this and win them adherents and allies. The Comintern agent Willi Münzenberg (later an influence on Dominic Cummings) was a master of manufacturing this kind of propaganda, in which realities were selected, distorted or suppressed altogether, and more favourable 'facts' were invented.

This attitude survived in the left in the post-war world. The truth was important to them only insofar as it confirmed their view of the world or the needs of some particular 'progressive' cause. It was especially on show in the protests of the Vietnam War, when the need to turn people against the war led the left to mythologise the Viet Cong and the Communist tyrant Ho Chi Minh.

Tony Blair's government was by no means alone in believing that it was allowed an exemption from the constraints of truth telling. But this belief led directly to calamity when New Labour peddled lies about Saddam Hussein's weapons of mass destruction in order to make the case for war against Iraq.

Blair's three immediate successors as prime minister – Gordon Brown, David Cameron and Theresa May – were capable of being devious. But this made them part of the pattern of worldly twentieth-century prime ministers like Harold Wilson and John Major. They were not habitual liars, and all three were driven (like Wilson and Major before them) by a sense of public duty and integrity.

Standards of truth telling, I will prove, collapsed at the precise moment Boris Johnson and his associates entered

10 Downing Street in the early afternoon of 24 July 2019. Before this moment, those engaged in public life could join in the national conversation regardless of what political tradition they hailed from or which party they supported. Afterwards they couldn't.

This is because, before July 2019, however strongly they disagreed with one another, there was a common standard of factual accuracy on which people of goodwill could agree. No longer. Truth – for nearly two centuries a powerful though sometimes muddy river running through the public domain – has been captured by the government and turned into a political weapon.

For centuries we have had an area of public discourse which belonged to everybody, a common ground where rival parties could coexist. Its extinction is a disaster. Political lying is a form of theft. It takes away people's democratic rights. Voters cannot make fair judgements on the basis of falsehoods. Truth has been taken out of the public domain. It's been privatised by the Johnson administration rather as Margaret Thatcher privatised water and electricity in the 1980s.

This means that lying, cupidity and lack of integrity have become essential qualities for ambitious ministers. Meanwhile public spirit, truth telling and scruple are an impediment to advancement. It has become all but impossible for an honest politician to survive, let alone flourish, in Boris Johnson's government.

How did this happen? The media are a part – though only

a part – of the explanation. Admittedly throughout their history British newspapers have disseminated many grotesque fabrications. But newspapers have also exposed the lies and venality of the rich and powerful. Indeed it has been part of their corporate myth, and their moral self-justification. But it was more than myth. For years and years, even popular and partisan publications prided themselves on being newspapers of record. They made efforts to verify what they were told.

In Chapter Seven I will show that when it came to Boris Johnson much of the press and media renounced that role. Britain's mainstream reporters and editors collectively turned a blind eye to the lies, misrepresentations and falsehoods promoted by Johnson and his ministers.

This was worse than negligence. Senior journalists facilitated, disseminated and collaborated with Johnson's lies. I will provide examples, name those responsible, cite some of the articles and expose the relationship with unnamed government 'sources'. Doing so will make me enemies. But without this it would be impossible to achieve the moral purpose of this book.

A great deal of political journalism has become the putrid public face of a corrupt government. There is only one good reason to be a journalist: to tell the truth. We should not go into our trade to become passive mouthpieces of politicians and instruments of their power. Too much of the media and political class have merged. The unnatural amalgamation has converted truth into falsehood, while lies have become truth.

It is at this point that the comparison between Boris Johnson and Donald Trump becomes especially haunting. Again and again, Britain and the United States have been driven by the same global currents. In the 1940s Winston Churchill and Franklin D. Roosevelt led the free world against fascist dictatorship. Ronald Reagan and Margaret Thatcher fought a common battle against Soviet tyranny. Two decades later Bill Clinton's New Democrats and Tony Blair's New Labour rebranded the left to create a softer capitalism on each side of the Atlantic.

Johnson and Trump find themselves joining in a common crusade against liberal democracy, and using lies and falsehood to fight their battles. They both believe that popular support ('the will of the people') gives them the legitimacy to take on elected chambers, the rule of law, the civil service, and also the political parties they lead.

This brings me on to the second theme of this book. Why should anyone care? Many voters shrug their shoulders. They make the cynical but false assumption that 'all politicians are the same'. This suits the cheats and liars because it means they escape invidious and damaging comparisons with the honest women and men who still populate the public stage.

Treating *all* politicians as liars is a gift to the ones who are. It induces cynicism and political apathy, on which they thrive. It licenses the destruction of the honour and integrity of British politics, a collapse that habitual liars such as Johnson are delighted to exploit. Cynicism lazily lumps virtuous public servants with charlatans, equates lies and truth, and makes political discourse meaningless. It denies voters even the possibility of seeking honest government at the ballot box.

But cynicism is not just lazy. It is dangerous. If history teaches one lesson it is this: we cannot enjoy freedom without truth, just as we cannot speak truth without freedom. And if we want to keep our freedoms, we can't let liars and cheats get away with it. This is because the liberal democracy we take for granted depends on a public domain with shared facts and assumptions upon which people of goodwill can agree. Once that public domain is ruined, truth ceases to be a point of communal reference. Instead it divides us. It becomes what power says it is. Those who doubt this should bear in mind what life is like in countries where power is concentrated in the hands of one individual or party and where there are no meaningful legal or democratic protections.

In Xi Jinping's China or Putin's Russia it's a crime *not to lie*. Criticism of the ruler is forbidden. Public conversation is reduced to a nightmare system of false statements and coded language where one word out of place can mean abduction, torture or death. Such regimes kill and torture truth tellers. Saudi Arabia sent a death squad to Istanbul where it murdered and then dismembered my magnificent former colleague Jamal Khashoggi,* a journalist whose

---

* We both wrote for *Middle East Eye*.

only offence was to make uncomfortable observations about the ruling family.

In Britain we have long prided ourselves that we do things differently. The law courts, Parliament, an impartial civil service and free press are part of a constitutional arrangement which for two centuries has prevented liars, charlatans, cheats and fascists from gaining power.

But we are in the process of abandoning the institutional protections that in the past have saved us from dictatorship. The Johnson government is set on a sustained, poisonous and calculated assault on these institutions. It's time we started to wonder why the Johnson administration finds the rule of law so disagreeable, and non-partisan civil service and parliamentary democracy an impediment to efficient government. Like a majority of the British people I voted for Brexit, but I did not vote for any of the above.

The Johnson government is convinced that after Brexit it has a special legitimacy sanctioned by the referendum vote. This means destroying the constitutional safeguards whose function is to protect British citizens from arbitrary rule. It also means turning on the civil service, whose core values of 'integrity, honesty, objectivity and impartiality'* are no longer viewed as fit for purpose. So I devote a section to Johnson's campaign against the Cabinet secretary, Sir Mark

---

* 'Civil Service values', Civil Service code, https://www.gov.uk/government/publications/civil-service-code/the-civil-service-code#civil-service-values.

Sedwill. As the most senior civil service post in Whitehall, the Cabinet secretary institutionally embodies the British values of impartiality, discretion, integrity, institutional conservatism. Those qualities are incompatible with the partisan method which Boris Johnson has imposed after becoming prime minister in July 2019.

A note on sources: books about lying, deception and falsehood in public life require especial care to be honest, transparent and fair. Every fact and assertion has therefore been backed up by a detailed footnote. These footnotes point to sources of information which can be checked by the reader. Many political journalists make use of private (and therefore uncheckable) sources. This practice is open to abuse, as I show in this book, and I make no use of such sources.

It is an especially serious matter to accuse someone of lying. This is because it involves such a damning and final judgement about character. Proven liars can never be trusted. Someone who lies once will lie again.

By contrast it is normal to make inadvertent false statements from time to time, out of a misunderstanding, ignorance or simply in the heat of the moment. Most of us have at some time used hyperbole or exaggerated language, or said something unfair about another person. Errors like these are forgivable, and can be forgotten once we have apologised and corrected the record.

This distinction means that it's important to define what we mean by a lie. The first test of a lie is that its user intends it to be believed. A lie may be uttered in the full knowledge that it is false or with complete indifference to its veracity (or as lawyers say, recklessness as to the truth). In either case it can contain an actual falsehood – but not always. It may for example involve a series of truthful statements but omit a piece of the jigsaw without which everything else is misleading (*suppressio veri*). Or it may place a series of individually true statements in such a relationship as to induce a false inference from them (*suggestio falsi*).

Above all, any kind of lie must also be *intended* to deceive. This judgement of motive makes the use of the term 'lie' especially hard. It involves looking into the workings of someone's mind and making a judgement. Ultimately only God can do that.

Take the case of Tony Blair. Blair continues to assert to this day that he never lied to the British people about Saddam Hussein's weapons of mass destruction ahead of the 2003 Iraq War. He accepts that he passed on false information about Saddam's weaponry in order to make the case for war. But he insists that he did this in good faith because he genuinely believed it was true.*

---

* 'Chilcot report: Read Tony Blair's full statement in response to the Iraq war inquiry', *The Independent*, 6 July 2016, https://www. independent.co.uk/news/uk/politics/chilcot-report-tony-blair-read-response-statement-in-full-iraq-war-inquiry-a7123251.html. As a lawyer Blair should know that the mere strength of a defendant's belief does not confer entitlement to any action taken in consequence and is therefore not a defence to a criminal charge. A man may sincerely believe that vicious aliens are about to attack him, but that does not

No one can ever challenge Blair about this until the day he goes on the public record and states that he knew that what he was saying at the time was nonsense. And he's unlikely to do that. Ultimately Blair is in the same position as the Kastom people in Vanuatu, who believe that Prince Philip is a divine being.* The Kastom people may well be mistaken, but it is unfair to challenge their good faith.

Unfortunately for Boris Johnson the Blair/Vanuatu defence does not work for him. Take his notorious 'inverted pyramid of piffle' denial that he was having an affair with a colleague at *The Spectator* magazine.† Here Johnson was not simply making a statement that contained a falsehood. He knew that the statement he was making was false.

Or take the claim repeatedly made by Johnson and senior colleagues during the 2019 general election that the government was building forty new hospitals (an episode I deal with in the next chapter). It's logical, though admittedly far-fetched, to claim in the prime minister's defence that when he first made the claim he genuinely believed that

---

justify firing an automatic weapon in their direction. A court will test first, whether it was reasonable in the circumstances for him to hold this belief and, second, whether firing the automatic weapon was a reasonable response.

* Maria E. Posse Emiliani, 'From the Caribbean to the South Pacific: Cultural Hybridity, Resistance, and Historical Difference', *ab-Original: Journal of Indigenous Studies and First Nations and First Peoples' Cultures* 1:1 (2017), pp. 62–80.

† Martin Fletcher, 'Inverted pyramid of piffle', *Tortoise*, 15 July 2019, https://members.tortoisemedia.com/2019/07/15/boris-brussels-edition/content.html.

his government was building forty hospitals even though the true number was (at most) six. But the prime minister's statement was rubbished by fact checkers, and he was asked about it by sceptical interviewers. He was surrounded by advisers in a position to put him right. Yet the prime minister went on repeating the claim about forty hospitals as the general election drew near. It's unreasonable to assume that Boris Johnson (along with Health Secretary Matt Hancock, who also made the claim) was suffering from a mental delusion.

Johnson and Hancock were lying, pure and simple, and I will say so in terms. Johnson has uttered many such lies. In the chapters which follow I shall analyse his methods, hold him to account, and spell out the consequences for all of us of his nightmare epistemological universe.

Chapter Two

THE 2019 ELECTION:
ONE LIE AFTER ANOTHER

'Well, they should be made to go on their knees through the chamber of the House of Commons, scourging themselves with copies of their offending documents which claim to prove one thing and actually prove something quite different.'

BORIS JOHNSON WHEN ASKED ON 6 DECEMBER 2019
HOW POLITICIANS WHO LIE TO THE PUBLIC
SHOULD BE PUNISHED

It's Friday lunchtime and the prime minister is on the election trail in Oldham. He's live on Sky News, speaking to supporters in front of the Tory battle bus. During a ten-minute speech, viewers learn that he is building forty new hospitals. It sounds a hugely impressive election pledge.

Actually it's a lie which the prime minister has already

repeated often during the campaign, and would go on to repeat on many more occasions. At best the government has only allocated money for six hospitals.* The prime minister tells viewers that '20,000 more police are operating on our streets to fight crime and bring crime down'.† This statement is also misleading. Recruitment will take place over three years and even if it happens will do no more than replace the drop in police numbers since the Conservatives came to power in 2010.‡

---

* Under Tory plans, six hospitals were allocated funding for rebuilding programmes between 2020 and 2025. Up to thirty-eight other hospitals would receive money to develop plans for upgrades between 2025 and 2030, but not to undertake any building work. For Johnson, the allocation of a small amount of funding, to initiate planning for improvements within an already existing hospital, which would only begin in five years' time, somehow equated to 'building' a new hospital. But no matter how many times this point was made by fact-checking organisations, opposition politicians and the media, Johnson and his government persisted with their lie, relying on a wilful misinterpretation of the facts to deceive. See 'Health Infrastructure Plan', Department of Health and Social Care, https://assets.publishing.service.gov.uk/government/uploads/system/uploads/attachment_data/file/835657/health-infrastructure-plan.pdf, p. 4. See also 'The government has given six hospitals money to upgrade buildings', Full Fact, 3 October 2019, https://fullfact.org/health/six-hospitals-not-forty.

† Johnson gave the speech in Oldham shortly before 1 p.m. on 15 November 2019; see Peter Oborne, 'It's not just Boris Johnson's lying. It's that the media let him get away with it', *The Guardian*, 18 November 2019, https://www.theguardian.com/commentisfree/2019/nov/18/boris-johnson-lying-media.

‡ Dan Sabbagh, 'Boris Johnson accused of misleading public over police numbers', *The Guardian*, 27 August 2019, https://www.theguardian.com/uk-news/2019/aug/27/boris-johnson-accused-of-misleading-public-over-police-numbers.

Boris Johnson then focuses on Jeremy Corbyn's 'plans to wreck the economy with a £1.2 trillion spending plan'. At this stage of the campaign, Labour's manifesto has not been published, let alone costed. Johnson's £1.2 trillion was a fabrication.*

The prime minister goes on to say that the Labour leader 'thinks home ownership is a bad idea and is opposed to it'. I have been unable to find evidence of Corbyn expressing this view. Perhaps Johnson is referring to a floated policy that would give 'right to buy' to private tenants.† The idea, which was only ever supposed to target the wealthiest landlords, was dropped and did not appear in the party's manifesto.‡ Johnson states that Jeremy Corbyn had made a speech calling for the abolition of British armed forces.§ A lie.

---

* As Full Fact concluded: 'Many of the figures behind this estimate are uncertain or based on flawed assumptions.' 'There are serious problems with the Conservatives' claim that Labour would spend £1.2 trillion', Full Fact, 19 November 2019, https://fullfact.org/news/conservative-claim-labour-1-trillion.

† Jim Pickard, 'UK's Labour would seize £300bn of company shares', *Financial Times*, 1 September 2019, https://www.ft.com/content/dc17d7ee-ccab-11e9-b018-ca4456540ea6.

‡ 'It's Time for Real Change: The Labour Party Manifesto 2019', https://labour.org.uk/wp-content/uploads/2019/11/Real-Change-Labour-Manifesto-2019.pdf.

§ Johnson was most likely referring to a speech made by the Labour leader in 2012 in which he said: 'Wouldn't it be wonderful if every politician around the world, instead of taking pride in the size of their armed forces, did what Costa Rica have done and abolished their army, and took pride in the fact they don't have an army?' It is clear from the full quote that Corbyn was describing a hypothetical situation and not advocating for the British armed services to be

At the end of his speech the Sky News presenter, Samantha Washington, does not challenge or correct any of Johnson's false statements. This inertia was a typical example of the media letting Johnson get away unchallenged with lies, falsehoods and fabrication.

I have been a political reporter for almost three decades and cut my teeth covering the 1992 general election won by John Major. I have never encountered a senior British politician who lies and fabricates so regularly, so shamelessly and so systematically as Boris Johnson. Or gets away with his deceit with such ease. Some of the election lies were tiny, but demonstrated that he would lie about anything at all. During a visit to a hospital he told doctors that he'd given up drink,* when only the previous day he'd been filmed sipping whisky on a visit to a distillery.† And he sipped beer on film the day after in a pub.‡

---

disbanded. In its 2019 manifesto Labour committed to spending 2 per cent of GDP on the armed forces. Nowhere does the manifesto say the party wants to disband the forces. (Dan Bloom, 'Here's what Jeremy Corbyn REALLY said about getting rid of the Army', *Mirror*, 14 September 2015, https://www.mirror.co.uk/news/uk-news/hereswhat-jeremy-corbyn-really-6438877; 'It's Time for Real Change'.

* 'General election: Boris Johnson reveals post-tipple Brexit booze ban', Sky News, 8 November 2019, https://news.sky.com/story/generalelection-boris-johnson-reveals-post-tipple-brexit-booze-ban-11857590.

† Tom Eden (@TomEden11), 'Boris Johnson indulging in some whisky tasting on his visit to an Elgin distillery', Twitter, 7 November 2019, https://twitter.com/TomEden11/status/1192479247211925504?s=20.

‡ 'Boris blows his "do or dry" pledge on campaign trail in Wolverhampton', ITV News, 11 November 2019, https://www.itv.com/news/central/2019-11-11/boris-blows-his-do-or-dry-pledge-on-campaign-trail-in-wolverhampton.

Interviewed by the *Sunday Times*, Johnson suggested that romance would bloom across the nation after Brexit was done, and added: 'There was a [baby boom] after the Olympics, as I prophesied in a speech in 2012. It was quite amazing. There was a big baby boom.'[*] I checked. There was no baby boom after the Olympics. In 2012, the year of the Olympics, there were 730,000 births in England and Wales. In 2013, the number was 699,000. The year–on–year fall of over 4 per cent was actually the greatest in thirty-eight years.[†]

He lied about the NHS throughout the election. Johnson's claim about forty new hospitals was part of a pattern. The prime minister told activists that the Tories were building a new hospital in the marginal seat of Canterbury.[‡] False – and cynical.[§] He misled local voters

---

[*] Tim Shipman, 'It's a Brexit! Boris Johnson predicts British baby boom', *Sunday Times*, 8 December 2019, https://www.thetimes.co.uk/article/its-a-brexit-boris-johnson-predicts-british-baby-boom-v93jqmjxp.

[†] 'Boris Johnson doesn't know how many kids were born under his watch', Full Fact, 8 December 2019, https://fullfact.org/electionlive/2019/dec/8/boris-johnson-baby-boom/.

[‡] Phil Hayes, 'Boris Johnson says Canterbury will get new hospital at Conservative Party Conference', KentOnline, 1 October 2019, https://www.kentonline.co.uk/canterbury/news/boris-johnson-says-kent-will-get-new-hospital-213260.

[§] Canterbury was not on the list of new hospitals the government had announced. The Department of Health the next day told KentOnline that while there was interest in a new hospital in Canterbury, there were no immediate plans for one (Paul Francis, 'Boris Johnson's Canterbury hospital claim downplayed by Department of Health',

with the assurance that 'we will certainly make sure that the A&E in Telford is kept open'.*

A trip to Whipps Cross hospital in east London generated one of Johnson's strangest lies. A man whose child was a patient at the hospital confronted the prime minister in a corridor in front of television cameras. 'The NHS has been destroyed,' the man said. 'And now you come here for a press opportunity.'†

As the cameras rolled, Johnson replied: 'Well, actually, there's no press here.'‡ The man, Omar Salem,

---

KentOnline, 2 October 2019, https://www.kentonline.co.uk/canterbury/news/boris-hospital-claim-downplayed-213326/.

* Under plans approved by Health Secretary Matt Hancock in October 2019, Telford's 24-hour A&E service would be downgraded and replaced with a so-called 'A&E Local' service only operating during 'core hours'. However, at the Conservative Party manifesto launch, Johnson told audiences: 'We will certainly make sure that the A&E in Telford is kept open.' Many took Johnson's words to mean that this plan would be scrapped. However, Hancock later told the *Shropshire Star* that 'we're going ahead with the plan and that's backing the decision that I published a month ago.' (Nick Humphreys, 'Chaos and confusion over Telford A&E as Boris comes to town', *Shropshire Star*, 25 November 2019, https://www.shropshirestar.com/news/politics/general-election-2019/2019/11/25/chaos-and-confusion-over-telford-ae-as-boris-comes-to-town.) Martin Wright, editor of the *Shropshire Star*, told me: 'For a moment it looked as if the A&E was saved. But then Matt Hancock clarified to say it would not be open full time.' He added: 'I am sure Mr Johnson would claim that we are keeping "A&E Local". But for those campaigning to save Telford's full-time A&E department, an "A&E Local" that is open during core hours is not the same as "saving the A&E".'

† Channel 4 News (@Channel4News), '"What do you mean there's no press here, who are these people?"', Twitter, 18 September 2019, https://twitter.com/Channel4News/status/1174300220571705344.

‡ Defenders of the prime minister might argue that technically he was correct in the sense that cameras but not writing press were there.

was incredulous.* 'What do you mean there's no press here?' he said, pointing at the cameras. 'Who are these people?'†

Johnson and his ministers repeatedly stated that plans for the NHS included 'the biggest increase in funding in living memory',‡ a figure of £34 billion. This was an especially disreputable lie because Tory ministers went on telling it even though it was disproved by experts. They pointed out that to compare Johnson's NHS funding pledge to past spending on the NHS requires taking account of inflation, which causes the value of the pound to fall year by year. Adjusted for inflation, the £34 billion comes down to

---

However, BuzzFeed uncovered a government communications briefing about Johnson's visit to the hospital, which included press quotes attributable to the prime minister. (Mark Di Stefano, 'Boris Johnson told the father of a sick child there was "no press" at a press opportunity arranged by Downing Street', BuzzFeed.News, 18 September 2019, https://www.buzzfeed.com/markdistefano/ boris-johnson-hospital-no-press.)

* Omar Salem later identified himself on social media as a 'Labour activist' (Patrick Worrall, 'FactCheck Q&A: what did Boris Johnson mean when he said there were "no press" at his hospital visit?', Channel 4 News, 20 September 2019, https://www.channel4.com/ news/factcheck/factcheck-qa-what-did-boris-johnson-mean-when-he-said-there-were-no-press-at-his-hospital-visit).

† Channel 4 News (@Channel4News), '"What do you mean there's no press here, who are these people?"'

‡ For example, Boris Johnson made the claim in an interview with Nick Ferrari on LBC: see 'Boris Johnson grilled by LBC listeners – watch in full', LBC/YouTube, 29 November 2019, https://youtu.be/ KTmpzuwgnDA.

£20.5 billion.* Not even close to the £24 billion a year spent on average by the Labour government up to 2009.†

Johnson lied systematically about political opponents. One of the targets was Nicola Sturgeon.‡ But the main attack was on the Labour leader, Jeremy Corbyn. Not content with falsely asserting that Corbyn wanted to dismantle the armed forces, Johnson went on the Andrew Marr show to claim the Labour leader had 'said he would disband MI5'.§ Marr did not demur, but to be sure I looked at the Labour manifesto. It contained no mention of MI5 but did pledge to 'ensure closer counter terrorism co-ordination between the police and the security services, combining neighbourhood expertise with international intelligence'.¶

---

* 'The £20.5 billion NHS England spending increase is the largest five year increase since the mid-2000s', Full Fact, 26 November 2019, https://fullfact.org/election-2019/nhs-spending-biggest-boost.

† Rachael Harker, 'NHS Expenditure', House of Commons Library, 17 January 2020, https://commonslibrary.parliament.uk/research-briefings/sn00724.

‡ For example, Boris Johnson claimed Nicola Sturgeon had said SNP policy was 'to join the euro'. He was referring to Sturgeon's interview with Andrew Neil, who asked about which currency an independent Scotland would use. At no point did Sturgeon say that Scotland would join the euro ('General election 2019: Nicola Sturgeon interview fact-checked', BBC News, 26 November 2019, https://www.bbc.co.uk/news/50552295). Indeed, the SNP repeatedly said it did not want Scotland to join the euro.

§ Dan Bloom, 'Boris Johnson falsely claims Jeremy Corbyn will scrap MI5 in live TV interview', *Mirror*, 1 December 2019, https://www.mirror.co.uk/news/politics/boris-johnson-falsely-claims-jeremy-21001911.

¶ 'It's Time for Real Change', p. 44.

Corbyn has never said he would disband M15.[*] Another lie.

The Conservative Party (though not Johnson himself, so far as I can tell) also claimed that Jeremy Corbyn had a 'plan for unlimited and uncontrolled immigration'[†] if he won the election. The due diligence website Fact Check judged that the claim was based on 'extreme assumptions' which were 'not credible'.[‡]

Boris Johnson said that Corbyn 'would whack corporation tax up to the highest in Europe'.[§] Not true. Labour had said it would raise the main rate of corporation tax to 26 per cent. This would not be anything like the highest in Europe. At the time of Johnson's claim, the rate of corporation tax in France was 31 per cent, and in Belgium the rate was 29 per cent.[¶] Johnson claimed meanwhile that cor-

---

[*] 'General Election 2019: Boris Johnson's interview with Andrew Marr fact-checked', BBC News, 1 December 2019, https://www.bbc.co.uk/news/election-2019-50624056.

[†] Hilary Osborne and Richard Partington, 'Revealed: Tory candidates issued with attack manuals on how to smear rivals', *The Guardian*, 28 November 2019, https://www.theguardian.com/politics/2019/nov/28/revealed-tory-candidates-issued-with-attack-manuals-on-how-to-smear-rivals.

[‡] 'Conservative claim about immigration under Labour is not credible', Full Fact, 16 November 2019, https://fullfact.org/election-2019/labour-free-movement-policy.

[§] Georgina Lee, 'Johnson wrong about Labour corporation tax', Channel 4 News, 18 November 2019, https://www.channel4.com/news/factcheck/factcheck-johnson-wrong-about-labour-corporation-tax.

[¶] 'Corporate tax rates table', KPMG, https://home.kpmg/xx/en/home/

poration tax in Britain was 'already the lowest in Europe'. This was also false.* Separately, he said that Corbyn would appease the SNP by holding a Scottish referendum in 2020 even though only two days earlier Corbyn had ruled out such a referendum.†

One of Johnson's lies was especially shameful. He said Corbyn's Labour 'point their fingers at individuals with a relish and a vindictiveness not seen since Stalin persecuted the kulaks'.‡ Stalin did much more than point his fingers at individuals. In December 1929 he announced a policy intended to liquidate an entire class of millions of people: the kulaks. *Kulak* was the pejorative Communist term for anyone in rural areas of the Soviet Union with a higher-than-average income through ownership of land, livestock and other assets, or simply better farming methods than their neighbours.

---

services/tax/tax-tools-and-resources/tax-rates-online/corporate-tax-rates-table.html.

* 'The ITV Boris Johnson vs Jeremy Corbyn debate, fact checked', Full Fact, 19 November 2019, https://fullfact.org/election-2019/itv-boris-johnson-jeremy-corbyn-debate-fact-checked.

† Alix Culbertson and Alan McGuinness, 'General election: Corbyn rows back on dismissal of second Scottish referendum', Sky News, 13 November 2019, https://news.sky.com/story/general-election-jeremy-corbyn-pledges-no-scottish-independence-referendum-in-first-term-as-pm-11860411.

‡ *Daily Telegraph*, 6 November 2019, p. 1; Gordon Rayner, 'Boris Johnson compares Jeremy Corbyn to Stalin for his 'hatred' of wealth creators as he launches election campaign', *The Telegraph*, 5 November 2019, https://www.telegraph.co.uk/politics/2019/11/05/boris-johnson-compares-jeremy-corbyn-stalin-hatred-wealth-creators.

Stalin's policy divided kulaks into three classes: those to be immediately shot or jailed, those to be deported to Siberia or other remote regions, and those to be evicted from their farms and used as local slave labour. The policy generated unintended mass famine as well as the regime's selective starvation. This was hidden from Western media and visitors, often with their collusion. The full total of avoidable premature deaths from Stalin's policy is probably in the tens of millions.[*]

Jeremy Corbyn did not threaten anyone with imprisonment, starvation or execution. At most, he intended to reduce Britain's billionaires to the status of multi-millionaires by taxation. To compare this to the persecution of the kulaks was to trash history and language, and insult all of Stalin's victims.

Johnson's inflammatory falsehood was emblazoned in large bold type over the front page of the *Daily Telegraph*. This is one of many examples of mainstream media complicity in amplifying Johnson's lies and falsehoods, a subject I will return to at length in Chapter Seven.

MORE LYING ABOUT RUSSIA

Russia haunted the general election. In late 2017 Parliament's Intelligence and Security Committee (ISC)

---

[*] See for one estimate Cynthia Haven, 'Stalin killed millions. A Stanford historian answers the question, was it genocide?', *Stanford News*, 23 September 2010, https://news.stanford.edu/2010/09/23/naimark-stalin-genocide-092310.

had launched an investigation into allegations of Russian interference into British politics.* This issue was especially embarrassing for the Conservatives because of reports that a number of wealthy business people with links to Vladimir Putin had given generously to the Tory party, as well as allegations of Russian interference in the 2016 Brexit referendum.†

The fifty-page report was completed by March 2019. It then went through the usual vetting and clearance with Whitehall and the intelligence agencies. The first stage involves fact checking. In the second stage, the committee and the intelligence services agree on redactions in the interest of national security. In the third stage, outstanding disagreements between the committee and the intelligence services are settled at a senior level. After all three stages were complete, the report was submitted to the prime minister on 17 October. There is no written protocol about the length of time the prime minister has to take to agree publication after receiving the final report, but the convention is that this takes ten working days.‡

---

* Daniel Kraemer, 'Russia report: When can we expect it to be published?', BBC News, 7 February 2020, https://www.bbc.com/news/uk-politics-51417880.

† Tom Harper and Caroline Wheeler, 'Russian Tory donors named in secret report', *Sunday Times*, 10 November 2019, https://www.thetimes.co.uk/article/russian-tory-donors-named-in-secret-report-z98nqpkx0.

‡ The chair of the committee tasked with carrying out the report, Dominic Grieve, told the Commons: 'It is a long-standing agreement

More than two weeks later, Michael Gove went on the *Today* programme. Asked about the delay in publication, he insisted: 'It's going through appropriate procedures, I think it's been lodged with No. 10 and it will be published in due course.'* But the ISC report had already gone through all the 'appropriate procedures'. It was being held up by the prime minister.

On *BBC Breakfast* the same day, Gove tried out another explanation: 'This is no different from the standard procedure, as I understand it, that occurs with these select committee reports.'† As a senior Cabinet minister, Gove was in a position to know that the 'standard procedure' was not being followed by Downing Street.

More than a week later, Rishi Sunak, then Treasury chief secretary (and now chancellor of the Exchequer), appeared on *Good Morning Britain*. He said: 'The nature of these reports is that they do contain sensitive information, which is why they need to go through an appropriate

that the Prime Minister will endeavour to respond within ten days.'
Hansard, HC Deb, 5 November 2019, vol. 667, col. 648.

* Aubrey Allegretti and Alan McGuinness, 'Russia meddling report: Government accused of cover-up as it refuses to release documents', Sky News, 5 November 2019, https://news.sky.com/story/michael-gove-refuses-to-explain-delay-on-report-into-russias-covert-action-in-britain-11854658.

† BBC Breakfast (@BBCBreakfast), 'Michael Gove MP denies on #BBCBreakfast that the Conservative Party are sitting on a report looking at alleged Russian interference in UK democracy', Twitter, 5 November 2019, https://twitter.com/bbcbreakfast/status/1191622213805527041.

period of vetting to make sure that they are safe to then be released. That's what's happened here.'* Sunak was not being straight with breakfast TV. By the time the report was submitted to Boris Johnson, it had already gone through the long period of due diligence with the intelligence services to ensure it was accurate and did not compromise national security.

Rishi Sunak's conduct highlights one of the unhappy consequences of having a liar as prime minister. Sunak, a young politician on the rise, was obliged to substantiate Boris Johnson's lies.† To contradict the official line would mean leaving the government.

Two weeks later, Boris Johnson was asked about the delayed report on an election edition of *Question Time*. He said: 'I see no reason to interfere with the normal timetable for these things.'‡ Johnson was lying to the *Question Time* audience and viewers. By refusing to publish the report, it was the prime minister himself who had failed to conform with the normal timetable for publishing ISC reports. He knew he was lying because

---

* 'Rishi Sunak on release timing of report into alleged Russian interference in the UK', *Good Morning Britain*/YouTube, 13 November 2019, https://youtu.be/YxlWwvFnNQo.

† Was Sunak himself lying? Impossible to be certain. It is possible he had been given a Conservative Party brief before going on the show, and most likely was relying on that.

‡ 'Boris Johnson defends stance on alleged Russian interference report', BBC News, 22 November 2019, https://www.bbc.co.uk/news/av/election-2019-50525394.

as prime minister he was responsible for the decision not to publish.*

BREXIT LIES

The prime minister's biggest lies involved Brexit. He repeatedly insisted that there would be no customs checks or controls for goods moving from Great Britain to Northern Ireland. This was an issue of exceptional gravity for any prime minister because border checks between Britain and Northern Ireland would compromise the integrity of the United Kingdom itself.

However, border checks became inevitable after Johnson struck his revised deal with Europe in October 2019. This left no ambiguity. Brexit Secretary Stephen Barclay informed Parliament in October that paperwork would be required for goods sent from Northern Ireland to Great Britain.† The Treasury noted that 'at a minimum, exit summary declarations will be required when goods are exported from NI to GB'.‡The government's own

---

* Dan Sabbagh, 'Boris Johnson urged to publish report on Russian meddling', *The Guardian*, 20 January 2020, https://www.theguardian.com/politics/2020/jan/20/boris-johnson-urged-to-publish-report-on-russian-meddling.

† Eleni Courea, 'UK Brexit secretary stumbles over detail of deal with EU', *Politico*, 21 October 2019, https://www.politico.eu/article/barclay-northern-irish-firms-to-complete-declarations-when-trading-with-britain.

‡ 'NI Protocol: Unfettered access to the UKIM', HM Treasury,

impact assessment on the withdrawal agreement stated: 'Goods moving from Great Britain to Northern Ireland will be required to complete both import declarations and Entry Summary (ENS) Declarations because the UK will be applying the EU's UCC (Union Custom Code) in Northern Ireland. This will result in additional administrative costs to businesses.'*

Boris Johnson, who had overseen negotiations and personally signed off the deal, knew all this. Yet he repeatedly stated the opposite. In Parliament on 22 October he said: 'There will be no checks between Great Britain and Northern Ireland.'† This bare-faced lie in all its moral squalor remains on the Commons order paper. Launching the Tory election campaign outside Downing Street two weeks later he told the nation: 'We can leave the EU as one UK, whole and entire and perfect as promised.' This from a prime minister who had told the Democratic Unionist Party conference the previous year that checks and customs controls between Great Britain and Northern Ireland would damage the 'fabric of the Union'.‡

---

available at https://www.politico.eu/wp-content/uploads/2019/12/LSRFUR-slides.pdf.

* Impact assessment, European Union (Withdrawal Agreement) Bill, 21 October 2019, https://assets.publishing.service.gov.uk/government/uploads/system/uploads/attachment_data/file/841245/EU_Withdrawal_Agreement_Bill_Impact_Assessment.pdf.

† Hansard, HC Deb, 22 October 2019, vol. 666, col. 835.

‡ Steerpike, 'Boris Johnson's speech to DUP conference: "we are on the verge of making a historic mistake"', *The Spectator*, 24 November

The lies continued. As the election approached, the prime minister told a pre-election press conference in Kent that 'there will be no checks on goods going from GB to NI and NI to GB because we are going to come out of the EU whole and entire. That was the objective we secured'.*
When Andrew Marr asked Johnson whether there would be tariffs and checks on goods moving from Northern Ireland into Great Britain after Brexit, the prime minister replied: 'Absolutely not.' When Marr put to Johnson that his own Brexit secretary, Stephen Barclay, had said there would be checks, Johnson insisted: 'There will be no tariffs and no checks.'†

During a TV debate with Jeremy Corbyn, moderator Julie Etchingham noted that Boris Johnson's deal would create 'a trade border down the Irish Sea'.‡ The prime minister replied: 'Not at all. Northern Ireland is part of the customs territory of the UK.' Johnson was correct to say Northern Ireland is part of the customs territory of

---

2018, https://www.spectator.co.uk/article/boris-johnson-s-speech-to-dup-conference-we-are-on-the-verge-of-making-a-historic-mistake.

* 'Boris Johnson denies Labour claim about Northern Ireland border checks', Sky News, 6 December 2019, https://news.sky.com/video/johnson-denies-labour-claim-about-brexit-northern-ireland-border-checks-11879551.

† Richard Partington, 'How accurate were Johnson's Andrew Marr interview claims?', *The Guardian*, 1 December 2019, https://www.theguardian.com/politics/2019/dec/01/how-accurate-were-boris-johnsons-assertions-on-andrew-marr.

‡ 'Johnson v Corbyn: The ITV Debate', ITV News/YouTube, 19 November 2019, https://youtu.be/9kEB5pqWpJw.

the UK. But his deal with Europe agreed that Northern Ireland would continue to follow many EU rules on food and manufactured goods, unlike the rest of the UK.

The prime minister's false and misleading statements about Northern Ireland were only part of the story. Johnson repeatedly claimed that Britain's continued membership of the EU costs an extra £1 billion a month.* That too was false.†

When reporter Michael Crick put to Johnson that he had led a referendum campaign which exploited fears about immigration from Turkey, Johnson replied: 'I didn't say anything about Turkey in the referendum campaign. I didn't say a thing about Turkey.' Pressed again, he added: 'I didn't make any remarks about Turkey, mate.'‡ Yet a week before the referendum in June 2016, Johnson wrote in a joint letter with his Vote Leave colleagues Michael Gove and Gisela Stuart: 'The only way to avoid having common borders with Turkey is to Vote Leave.'§

---

* Hansard, HC Deb, 28 October 2019, vol. 667, col. 54.

† 'It's not true to say a Brexit extension would cost £1 billion', Full Fact, 1 October 2019, https://fullfact.org/europe/1-billion-brexit-extension.

‡ 'Boris denies making any claims about Turkey in the referendum campaign', *Daily Mail*/YouTube, 18 January 2019, https://youtu.be/7N3VbS-iw44.

§ 'Letter to the Prime Minister and Foreign Secretary – Getting the facts clear on Turkey', Vote Leave, 16 June 2016, http://www.voteleavetakecontrol.org/letter_to_the_prime_minister_and_foreign_secretary_getting_the_facts_clear_on_turkey.html.

The 2019 general election was held on the eve of Brexit, the most momentous event in post-war British history. Yet Johnson's Brexit fabrications were not held up to serious inspection by the media at any stage.

DELIBERATE AND SYSTEMATIC DECEIT

It is sometimes said that British politicians can be divided into vicars and bookmakers and voters prefer the latter.* Johnson falls into the bookmaker class. Voters enjoy his good humour and low tricks. They let him get away with anything. He charms them and it feels innocent fun. One reason why Boris Johnson gets away with lying is that so many voters like him.†

Yet most of Johnson's general election lies were not innocent. They were part of a deliberate and carefully calculated strategy of deception. As the general election got under way, the Conservative Research Department (CRD) prepared an election campaign political brief as a guide for candidates

---

* Journalist Malcolm Muggeridge first made the comparison: 'To succeed pre-eminently in English public life it is necessary to conform either to the popular image of a bookie or of a clergyman.' See Antony Jay (ed.), *Oxford Dictionary of Political Quotations*, 3rd ed. (Oxford: Oxford University Press, 2006), p. 221.

† According to YouGov, Boris Johnson is the most popular Conservative politician and the most famous. He is described by fans as conservative, confident, humorous, admirable and intelligent (https://yougov.co.uk/topics/politics/explore/public_figure/ Boris_Johnson).

with attack lines and policy guidance in public meetings and door-to-door canvassing.[*] The CRD document contained a series of false claims, including many of those relentlessly used by Boris Johnson during the election: the forty new hospitals;[†] record spending rise on the NHS;[‡] Corbyn's £1.2 trillion in extra spending;[§] Labour's 'uncontrolled and unrestricted immigration' policy;[¶] and others.[**]

The Conservative Party adopted the same strategy of deliberately spreading lies and falsehoods on social media. The Conservatives launched an advertising blitz on Facebook between 1 and 4 December as the general election approached, running nearly 7,000 advertisements targeted at swing voters and marginal constituencies.[††] Of these, no less than 88 per cent had *already* been criticised or denounced as misleading by independent fact-checking organisations.[‡‡]

---

[*] Osborne and Partington, 'Revealed: Tory candidates issued with attack manuals on how to smear rivals'.

[†] *Political Brief: General Election 2019*, Conservative Research Department, 14 November 2019, p. 8.

[‡] Ibid., p. 8.

[§] Ibid., p. 7.

[¶] Ibid., p. 7.

[**] Osborne and Partington, 'Revealed: Tory candidates issued with attack manuals on how to smear rivals'.

[††] Alastair Reid and Carlotta Dotto, 'Thousands of misleading Conservative ads side-step scrutiny thanks to Facebook policy', First Draft, 6 December 2019, https://firstdraftnews.org/latest/thousands-of-misleading-conservative-ads-side-step-scrutiny-thanks-to-facebook-policy.

[‡‡] Ibid.

Indeed, the Tory Party social media strategy was generally dishonest. For example, it deliberately doctored footage of the shadow Brexit secretary, Sir Keir Starmer (today Labour leader), to make it look as if he was at a loss for words when asked by Piers Morgan about Labour's Brexit position.* In fact, Starmer had answered the question immediately, confidently and fluently.† The Conservative Party appeared to have edited the footage by taking a segment in which Starmer was listening to a question and inserting it after Morgan's question. The video was a deliberate attempt to mislead voters.‡

A comparable moment occurred during the ITV leadership debate on 19 November when the official Conservative press office Twitter account changed its

---

* Conservatives (@Conservatives), 'WATCH: Jeremy Corbyn's Brexit Minister can't or won't answer a simple question about Labour's position on Brexit', Twitter, 5 November 2019, https://twitter.com/conservatives/status/1191686313461846016?lang=en.

† 'Keir Starmer quizzed on Labour's policies if successful in general election', *Good Morning Britain*/YouTube, 5 November 2019, https://youtu.be/VW9VS47cjrw.

‡ In a TV interview the following day, Morgan put it to Tory chairman James Cleverly that the video was 'fake news'. Morgan said: 'Why should we believe any video or anything that you guys put out? If you're prepared to be that shameless and that cynical and that misleading, why should we believe anything?' Cleverly did not answer the question and refused to apologise for the video. 'Piers presses James Cleverly on the Tory Party "doctored" video of Keir Starmer', *Good Morning Britain*/YouTube, 6 November 2019, https://youtu.be/3iJ5uqdpEm0.

name to @factcheckUK.* Under its new, apparently non-partisan title, it stated that claims made by Johnson were true and claims made by Corbyn were false. Here again Boris Johnson's Conservative Party was deliberately deceiving voters by presenting party propaganda as independently verified facts. Foreign Secretary Dominic Raab defended the Tory Party's fake Twitter account by saying that 'no one gives a toss about the social media cut and thrust'.†

This remark was an obvious lie. Social media was at the heart of Tory Party general election strategy. Figures from the Electoral Commission reveal that the Conservatives spent £2.1 million on Facebook advertising alone during the 2017 election campaign.‡ In comparison, Labour spent £577,000. In the 2019 election, the Conservatives spent over a million pounds on Facebook advertisements and a further £1.76 million on Google advertisements, plus more than £100,000 for a single advert at the top of YouTube's

---

* Dave Lee, 'Election debate: Conservatives criticised for renaming Twitter profile "factcheckUK"', BBC News, 20 November 2019, https://www.bbc.co.uk/news/technology-50482637.

† 'Dominic Raab on "factcheckUK": "No-one gives a toss about social media cut and thrust"', BBC News, 20 November 2019, https://www.bbc.co.uk/news/av/uk-politics-50487624/dominic-raab-on-factcheckuk-no-one-gives-a-toss-about-social-media-cut-and-thrust.

‡ Peter Walker, 'Tories spent £18.5m on election that cost them majority', *The Guardian*, 19 March 2018, https://www.theguardian.com/politics/2018/mar/19/electoral-commission-conservatives-spent-lost-majority-2017-election.

homepage in the final days of the campaign.* The sums spent show that the Conservative Party cares very much about the social media cut and thrust.

There is irrefutable evidence that Conservative Party lies and distortions in the 2019 election were cynical, systematic and prepared in advance. Johnson's Conservatives deliberately set out to lie and to cheat their way to victory. The strategy triumphed.

---

* Katharine Dommett and Sam Power, 'Democracy in the Dark: Digital Campaigning in the 2019 General Election and Beyond', Electoral Reform Society, September 2019, https://www. electoral-reform.org.uk/latest-news-and-research/publications/ democracy-in-the-dark-digital-campaigning-in-the-2019-general-election-and-beyond/#sub-section-4.

Chapter Three

THE TRIUMPH OF
POLITICAL LYING

'The Catholic and the Communist are alike in
assuming that an opponent cannot be both honest
and intelligent.'

GEORGE ORWELL

Twenty years ago, I met John Profumo when we both
spoke at a charity event. He was a softly spoken, slightly
built, understated man who carried himself with dignity
and distinction. This struck me because all I knew about
Profumo was that he had been at the heart of Britain's most
notorious political scandal of the post-war era.

When he died not long afterwards, I studied his
obituaries. As an MP he had been part of the May
1940 Conservative Party revolt that destroyed Neville
Chamberlain and established Winston Churchill in

10 Downing Street.* In fact, he was the last survivor of the Conservative MPs who saved their country. The following day the chief whip, David Margesson, took him aside: 'I can tell you this, you utterly contemptible little shit. On every morning that you wake up for the rest of your life you will be ashamed of what you did last night.'†

John Profumo went on to serve throughout the Second World War, was mentioned in dispatches during the fighting in north Africa and was awarded an OBE in 1944 'in recognition of gallant and distinguished service in Italy' as a staff officer.‡ After the war he rose steadily and had reached the rank of war secretary when calamity struck. Profumo embarked on an affair with Christine Keeler, a 19-year-old model who, unluckily for him, was also involved with the Soviet navy attaché, Yevgeny Ivanov.§

The matter was raised on the floor of the Commons. Profumo denied any 'impropriety',¶ but resigned when this turned out to be false. He retired and devoted himself to charity work. Thirty years later, Margaret Thatcher

---

* 'Obituary: John Profumo', BBC News, 10 March 2006, http://news. bbc.co.uk/1/hi/uk_politics/1158516.stm.

† Roy Jenkins, *Churchill: A Biography* (London: Pan, 2002), p. 583.

‡ *London Gazette*, 21 December 1944, available at https://www. thegazette.co.uk/London/issue/36850/supplement/5843.

§ See Richard Davenport-Hines, *An English Affair: Sex, Class and Power in the Age of Profumo* (London: William Collins, 2013).

¶ Hansard, HC Deb, 22 March 1963, vol. 674, cols 809–10.

invited him to her 70th birthday dinner, where he was placed on the right hand of the Queen.* Profumo was the paradoxical embodiment of a governing system where integrity counted. Misleading the Commons was regarded with special horror.

Erskine May, the authoritative procedural manual for Parliament, still warns members not to do this, in Paragraph 15.27, which reads:

> The Commons may treat the making of a deliberately misleading statement as a contempt. In 1963, the House resolved that in making a personal statement which contained words which they later admitted not to be true, a former Member had been guilty of a grave contempt.
>
> In 2006, the Committee on Standards and Privileges concluded that a Minister who had inadvertently given a factually inaccurate answer in oral evidence to a select committee had not committed a contempt, but should have ensured that the transcript was corrected. The Committee recommended that they should apologise to the House for the error.†

---

* David Tang, 'Softer side of the Iron Lady', *Financial Times*, 12 April 2013, https://www.ft.com/content/6acd32ba-a1cd-11e2-ad0c-00144feabdc0

† 'Members deliberately misleading the House', Erskine May, https://erskinemay.parliament.uk/section/5022/members-deliberately-misleading-the-house.

Meanwhile the Ministerial Code insists: 'It is of paramount importance that Ministers give accurate and truthful information to Parliament, correcting any inadvertent error at the earliest opportunity. Ministers who knowingly mislead Parliament will be expected to offer their resignation to the Prime Minister.'*

But Erskine May and the Ministerial Code are now ignored. Ministers (including the prime minister) lie and cheat with impunity. Their falsehoods remain contemptuously uncorrected on the official Hansard record. That is why I felt compelled to write this book: to attempt to explain the destruction and collapse of the twentieth-century code of public integrity.

It had survived for several decades after Profumo's departure. Prime ministers were often accused by political opponents of dishonesty. But these allegations were rhetorical, very rarely substantiated, and often hypocritical.

It is also important to understand that the rule against lying did not always apply. It was always recognised that there were exceptions. As a reporter for the London *Evening Standard* in March 1994, I was dispatched to hear the Conservative minister William Waldegrave give evidence to the Treasury and Civil Service Committee. I heard him tell MPs that 'in exceptional circumstances, it is necessary

---

* 'Ministerial accountability to Parliament', Erskine May, https:// erskinemay.parliament.uk/section/4569/ministerial-accountability-to-parliament.

to say something that is untrue to the House of Commons. The House of Commons understands that and accepts that.'

I dashed out of the committee room, charged upstairs, picked up the phone to the news desk and filed. My story made the splash in later editions, and dominated Fleet Street's front pages the following day, creating a short-lived sensation. Waldegrave's comments (or an inaccurate version of them) even made it into a dictionary of quotations.* I felt a bit guilty about this. In the uproar, Waldegrave was held up as at worst a scoundrel, at best a naïve fool. In fact, he was one of the most scrupulous politicians, not just of the modern but of any era. It was agonised honesty and not cynical depravity that led him to make his statement that ministers were sometimes (in very rare and constrained circumstances) entitled to lie. If anybody was guilty of lying, it was Waldegrave's critics.

Lord Waldegrave describes this incident in his autobiography (he calls me 'clever if erratic', which was half right) and sticks by his guns: 'Truth telling is a moral imperative, but it may clash with some other moral imperative; so, just occasionally, it might be wrong to tell the truth.' He also recalls that in the aftermath of the controversy he received a letter. It came from 'an old gentleman who had been serving on a battleship as a young rating in early 1940 when Churchill had come aboard as First Lord of the Admiralty.

---

* Gyles Brandreth (ed.), *Oxford Dictionary of Humorous Quotations*, 5th ed. (Oxford: Oxford University Press, 2013), p. 181.

Put in a group to question the great man, he had nervously asked, "Is everything you tell us true?" The answer, he alleged, was: "Young man, I have told many lies for my country, and will tell many more."*

Lies are often (though not always) justified in wartime. Few would dispute the necessity for the elaborate deception operation overseen by Churchill to fool German high command ahead of the D-Day landings in 1944. They are also occasionally acceptable in peacetime. The example cited by Waldegrave involved Jim Callaghan, who in the autumn of 1967 is held to have ruled out the devaluation of sterling he knew to be imminent because he wished to avoid a run on sterling, which would have cost the Bank of England a fortune.

TONY BLAIR'S LIES

Nevertheless, when Callaghan became prime minister he cared about integrity. Contrary to claims made by opponents, so did his successors Margaret Thatcher and John Major.

This changed with Tony Blair. When he became prime minister in 1997, he brought with him into 10 Downing Street a dislike of candour and a structural preference for deceit that remained a hallmark of his leadership until

---

* William Waldegrave, *A Different Kind of Weather: A Memoir* (London: Constable, 2015), pp. 203–4.

he left office ten years later.* This dishonesty defined his relationship with the Labour Party, with the British people and with Whitehall. Eventually Blair used a lie, Saddam Hussein's weapons of mass destruction, as the pretext to drag Britain to war with Iraq.† As time went on, he began to occupy a parallel reality. Even thirteen years after the Iraq invasion, the former British prime minister continued to insist that he was right to order the invasion of Iraq, telling a press conference in 2016: 'I believe we made the right decision and the world is better and safer.'‡

As with Boris Johnson, Blair's lies to Parliament remain uncorrected on the Hansard record, in defiance of the Ministerial Code.§ I was a political reporter throughout the Blair premiership and raised the question of New Labour deceit with many of his aides and ministers. They told me the

---

* I set out Tony Blair's record in detail in *The Rise of Political Lying* (London: Free Press, 2005).

† See ibid.

‡ Luke Harding, 'Tony Blair unrepentant as Chilcot gives crushing Iraq war verdict', *The Guardian*, 6 July 2016, https://www.theguardian.com/uk-news/2016/jul/06/chilcot-report-crushing-verdict-tony-blair-iraq-war.

§ For example, Blair's false claim that the intelligence that Saddam possessed weapons of mass destruction was 'extensive, detailed and authoritative' remains on the parliamentary record nearly two decades after it was made (Hansard, HC Deb, 24 September 2002, vol. 390, col. 3). See also Blair's speech to the House of Commons on the eve of the war, 18 March 2003, for choice examples of a prime minister misleading Parliament. I deal with lying over Iraq in detail in *The Rise of Political Lying*, pp. 184–221. My *Not the Chilcot Report* (London: Head of Zeus, 2016) deals in detail with the run-up to the Iraq War.

same thing: Labour had been in opposition for eighteen years before the election victory of 1997. They felt (with good reason) that a venal Tory-supporting press had distorted, misrepresented and often lied about Labour policy. So Blair and his advisers felt there was no way that Labour would win power, let alone retain it, if it relied on telling the truth.

They also told me Labour believed that it was virtuous and sought power not for itself but in order to serve the British people. This gave the party, so Blair loyalists believed, a plausible moral justification for telling the lies that were needed to keep it in power. In this it followed the example of Tony Blair's friend and political hero Bill Clinton. Interestingly, Clinton too was scarred by rough media handling in the early 1980s, during his first term as governor of Arkansas, which ended in electoral defeat. Clinton returned to power determined never to lose it again. He learnt (and later taught Blair) the art of 'triangulation', being politically equidistant from all bodies of opinion on any controversial topic. This in turn led him to construct a constantly moving narrative of his positions and policies, and their outcomes, one sometimes untethered by objective reality. Clinton's methods worked. He stayed in power, became a good governor of his state, gained national attention and, of course, became a superlatively persuasive challenger for the presidency.*

---

* See Garry Wills's assessment of his methods in 'The Clinton Principle', *New York Times Magazine*, 19 January 1997, https://www.nytimes.com/1997/01/19/magazine/the-clinton-principle.html.

Both Clinton and Blair sincerely believed that they were fighting for good causes in their political careers, and that this overrode their obligation to tell the whole truth on any issue. I do not doubt the sincerity of Tony Blair and some (though probably not all) of his supporters. However, the belief that Blair and New Labour had a special dispensation to ignore the truth in a noble purpose gave a licence to any successor to do the same out of pure self-interest. Tony Blair paved the way for Boris Johnson, who has created a new epistemological universe.

By the time the Blair premiership ended in 2007, I had got in the habit of keeping a file of political lies. My file shows that Blair's successors Gordon Brown, David Cameron and Theresa May were capable of subterfuge, though not remotely on the scale of Tony Blair. All three prime ministers were driven by a sense of duty, and keenly aware of the difference between truth and falsehood.

Not so Boris Johnson. As a liar he cannot be compared to Tony Blair. He has never needed a noble justification for lying. He lies habitually, with impunity, and without conscience. This puts his dishonesty into the same category as Donald Trump's. Although far below Trump's in scale and stridency, it is epic by British standards.

The Lies and Falsehoods of Trump and Johnson

Superficially the US president and the British prime minister could hardly be less alike: a classically educated Old Etonian and a brash New York property developer. Yet the gulf isn't as great as it seems. Both men are noted for making outlandish claims which have little or no connection with reality. They are licensed to enjoy irregular private lives which would ruin conventional politicians. Though both members of the financial, social and political elite, they lead populist movements.

They lie in many of the same ways. Bill Clinton and Tony Blair thought their lies were justified because they were in a good cause. That's not true of Boris Johnson and Donald Trump. They lie with humour and relish. They invent damaging falsehoods about political opponents, whether it be Johnson's unsupported assertion that Jeremy Corbyn wanted to dismantle the British armed forces or Trump's repeated claim that Barack Obama was born in Kenya.* Johnson does his best to preserve a cheery, benign image by getting others to spread lies and smears about his opponents while keeping his own hands clean (a technique I will explore more deeply in

---

* During the 2012 election campaign, Donald Trump often hinted that President Obama had secretly been born in Kenya, and his birth certificate was fraudulent.

Chapter Seven), while Trump enjoys doing the dirty work himself.

They've reached the top despite the profound distrust of colleagues, sinister connections on the far right, a record of racism and long records of cheating and fabrication which had become apparent well before they reached the highest office. Both are lazy. Neither bothers with detail. Both flourish in a world of illusion and made-up facts. Johnson's dishonesty, though marked, is not as flagrant as Trump's. He is Trump's genteel country cousin, able to sugar-coat his lies with the legacy of an expensive classical education.

Above all, Johnson and Trump turned themselves into popular entertainers who possess the irreplaceable art of arresting the attention of voters. In the next two chapters I will compare the lies and falsehoods of the former United States president and the British prime minister.

Chapter Four

BRITAIN'S FIRST GONZO
PRIME MINISTER

'One believes in them as one believes in characters in a
soap: one accepts the invitation to half believe in them.'

BERNARD WILLIAMS

Twenty-five years ago, the Cambridge philosopher Bernard
Williams wrote a prophetic essay about the emergence of
an arresting new public discourse. Williams noted that
political leaders

> certainly appear before the public and make claims about
> the world and each other. However, the way in which these
> people are presented, particularly if they are prominent,
> creates to a remarkable degree an impression that they are
> in fact characters in a soap opera being played by people
> of the same name.

They are called by their first names or have the same kind of jokey nicknames as soap opera characters. The same broadly sketched personalities, the same dispositions to triumphs and humiliations, which are schematically related to the doings of the other characters. When they reappear, they give off the same impression of remembering only just in time to carry on from where they left off and they equally disappear into the script of the past after something else more interesting has come up. It would not be right to say that when one takes the view of these people that is offered in the media, one does not believe in them. One believes in them as one believes in characters in a soap: one accepts the invitation to half believe in them.*

Williams, writing in 1996, was describing the precise environment which fostered Boris Johnson and Donald Trump.

The Cambridge philosopher had made his early reputation bringing back morality to the study of moral philosophy, which had become an arid and technical subject in the post-war era. His final substantial work attacked the prevalent notion in the academic world that there was no such thing as truth.† Williams's concern with morality enabled him to understand, at an early stage, that fact was mutating into fiction and vice versa.

---

* Bernard Williams, 'Truth, Politics, and Self-Deception', *Social Research* 63:3 (1996), pp. 603–17.

† Bernard Williams, *Truth and Truthfulness: An Essay in Genealogy* (Princeton: Princeton University Press, 2002).

Political correspondents were much slower to compre-hend this change, let alone its consequences, which is why we have been such useless guides to the great upheavals of recent years: above all, the rise of Trump and the Brexit vote. There was little hope for conventional politicians like Jeremy Hunt (the candidate beaten by Johnson in the struggle for the Tory leadership) or Hillary Clinton in the United States.

Johnson and Trump had stumbled on a new way of doing politics. They intuitively understood how to put into practice the insight which Williams had worked out in his ivory tower twenty years before: 'The status of politics as represented in the media is ambiguous between entertain-ment and the transmission of discoverable truth.' The rules had changed.

THE EARLY CAREER OF BORIS JOHNSON

Johnson was twenty-three when he was first sacked for lying.* This early setback stemmed from the discov-ery of the ruins of a fourteenth-century palace built by Edward II on the banks of the Thames. Johnson, a trainee on *The Times*, was instructed to write about it. He rang up his godfather, the Oxford academic Colin Lucas. Lucas was quoted in Johnson's article saying that while at the

---

* Sonia Purnell, *Just Boris: The Irresistible Rise of a Political Celebrity* (London: Aurum, 2011), pp. 180–90.

palace Edward had 'enjoyed a reign of dissolution with his catamite'.*

As so often with Johnson, the facts did not support his claims. The palace on the Thames was not built until 1325, while King Edward's alleged catamite (Piers Gaveston) had been beheaded thirteen years earlier. Incidentally, a catamite refers to a boy kept by an older man: Gaveston and Edward were the same age. Boris Johnson had fabricated the Lucas quote. Johnson then made matters worse: 'I wrote a further story saying that the mystery had deepened about the date of the castle.'† Johnson's editor, Charles Wilson, had backed his reporter after the first story. The second time he sacked him. It is worth noting the nature of the story, a distant piece of history, interesting but with no present political or other significance. But *The Times* then still prided itself on being a journal of record and Johnson had to go.

The future British prime minister crossed the street to the *Daily Telegraph*, which quickly made him Brussels correspondent, normally a dead-end appointment in a city notorious for dull, bureaucratic stories. Johnson made his reputation. He stumbled upon a new form of journalism

---

* Maurice Chittenden, 'Reporter Boris: you couldn't make it up', *Sunday Times*, 10 September 2006, https://www.thetimes.co.uk/article/reporter-boris-you-couldnt-make-it-up-7k9l7r9nwgz.

† 'My greatest mistake: Boris Johnson, MP for Henley and editor of *The Spectator*', *The Independent*, 21 May 2002, https://www.independent.co.uk/news/media/my-greatest-mistake-boris-johnson-mp-for-henley-and-editor-of-the-spectator-189322.html.

which thirty years later would become famous as fake news. He reported that the EU wanted to ban prawn cocktail crisps.* He filed a sensational story on plans to blow up the Berlaymont building, headquarters of the European Commission.† The Berlaymont still stands today, three decades later, and prawn cocktail crisps are still available for sale.

Johnson told *Telegraph* readers that the Berlaymont was to be replaced by a 'kilometre-high skyscraper topped by a communications mast'.‡ It wasn't. That Brussels harboured plans to monitor smelly European farmyards,§ to standardise coffin sizes.¶ None of these plans, if they existed in the first place, ever came to fruition.

---

* Boris Johnson, 'I'm no longer Nasty, but please stop lying about Nice', *The Telegraph*, 17 October 2002, https://www.telegraph. co.uk/comment/personal-view/3582944/Im-no-longer-Nasty-but-please-stop-lying-about-Nice.html.

† Rory Watson, 'Berlaymont is still here, Boris notwithstanding', 3 July 2019, https://www.ft.com/content/4a83c72e-9cf5-11e9-b8ce-8b459ed04726.

‡ Karla Adam and William Booth, 'Former colleagues of Boris Johnson as a journalist, warn he is "not fit for national office"', *Independent*, 22 July 2020, https://www.independent.co.uk/news/uk/politics/boris-johnson-telegraph-times-journalist-thatcher-tory-leadership-churchill-a9014196.html.

§ Martin Fletcher, 'Boris Johnson peddled absurd EU myths – and our disgraceful press followed his lead', *New Statesman*, 1 July 2016, https://www.newstatesman.com/politics/uk/2016/07/boris-johnson-peddled-absurd-eu-myths-and-our-disgraceful-press-followed-his.

¶ Peter Barnes, 'Reality Check: Does the EU limit coffin sizes?', BBC News, 23 March 2016, https://www.bbc.co.uk/news/uk-politics-eu-referendum-35886338.

Johnson told *Telegraph* readers that Brussels posed a threat to British pink sausages.* That it wanted to standardise condom sizes because Italians had smaller penises (in fact the EU was concerned about the safety of condoms, not their size, and the work had been carried out by the European Committee for Standardization, which is not even part of the EU).† That 'the European Commission wants to count every field and farm animal under a Domesday Book-style survey aimed at preventing fraud following fundamental reform of the Common Agricultural Policy'.‡

These stories typically contained a grain of truth, but were in essence fabrications. Martin Fletcher, who worked as Brussels correspondent for *The Times* (a rival paper), later listed many of them on the *Tortoise* news website. He noted a common theme because they 'invariably portrayed "Brussels" as a den of conspirators determined to create a European superstate which would destroy Britain's sovereignty, traditions and way of life'.§ Fletcher also wrote that 'they helped

---

* Sarah Helm, 'Brussels chuckles as reality hits mythmaker', *The Independent*, 23 July 1995, https://www.independent.co.uk/news/uk/home-news/brussels-chuckles-as-reality-hits-mythmaker-1592828.html.

† Jennifer Rankin and Jim Waterson, 'How Boris Johnson's Brussels-bashing stories shaped British politics', *The Guardian*, 14 July 2019, https://www.theguardian.com/politics/2019/jul/14/boris-johnson-brussels-bashing-stories-shaped-politics.

‡ Fletcher, 'Inverted pyramid of piffle'.

§ Ibid.

ignite the simmering euro-scepticism of the Conservative right. They also set the tone for much of the rest of British journalism, which found Johnson's cartoon caricature of Brussels much more appealing than the real thing'.*

Conrad Black, then the proprietor of the *Telegraph*, agrees. As Johnson prepared to enter Downing Street in the summer of 2019, Black wrote a generous defence of Johnson in *The Spectator*, arguing that he 'was such an effective correspondent for us in Brussels that he greatly influenced British opinion on this country's relations with Europe'.†

If Black is correct, Johnson's juvenile journalism from the early 1990s should be credited with creating a new genre which over time led to the national mood of ridicule and suspicion towards Europe which played a part in the Brexit vote a quarter of a century later – and thus Johnson's premiership. Not everyone liked the joke. When Johnson left Brussels, the *Times* reporter James Landale adapted Hilaire Belloc's 'Matilda': 'Boris told such dreadful lies / It made one gasp and stretch one's eyes.'‡

Johnson was sacked for lying for a second time in 2004. By then he was simultaneously editor of *The Spectator*, Tory

---

* Ibid. I am indebted to Martin Fletcher for his list of Johnson's fabrications.

† Conrad Black, 'Battle of Hastings: Max's campaign against Boris is cowardly', *The Spectator*, 29 June 2019, https://www.spectator.co.uk/article/battle-of-hastings.

‡ Sam Knight, 'The empty promise of Boris Johnson', *New Yorker*, 13 June 2019, https://www.newyorker.com/magazine/2019/06/24/the-empty-promise-of-boris-johnson.

MP for Henley (having falsely assured Black that he would never become an MP while *Spectator* editor*) and a shadow minister. Amid this confusion of roles, Johnson was confronted with tabloid allegations that he was in an affair with a colleague, which he described as 'complete balderdash' and 'an inverted pyramid of piffle'.† Tory leader Michael Howard sacked Johnson,‡ causing *The Guardian* to announce 'an end to an unlikely but uniquely engaging political career'.§

---

* Johnson was offered the role by Black on the condition that he gave up his political ambitions. However, he soon became Conservative MP for Henley. Dan Sabbagh and Frances Perraudin, 'Laughter and lies: Johnson's journey from journalist to MP', *The Guardian*, 15 July 2019, https://www.theguardian.com/politics/2019/jul/15/laughter-lies-boris-johnson-journey-journalist-mp.

† 'Boris Johnson's regret at sacking', BBC News, 14 November 2004, http://news.bbc.co.uk/1/hi/uk_politics/4010293.stm. Cahal Milmo, 'Tory front bench split over Howard's show of strength', *Independent*, 15 November 2004, https://www.independent.co.uk/news/uk/politics/tory-front-bench-split-over-howards-show-of-strength-533269.html.

‡ Howard sacked Johnson for lying to his communications director about the affair. Amid speculation that he voted for Johnson during the 2019 Tory leadership election, the former Tory leader told the *Today* programme that Johnson had not lied directly to him. Howard said: 'First of all, he wasn't in the Shadow Cabinet. It's often said that he lied to me. He didn't lie to me. What happened was that my director of communications at the time was convinced that Boris had lied to him, and strongly advised me that I should take the action which I took.' He added: 'I took that action, I'm not entirely sure that I was right to take that action, but I'm happy to set the record straight.' (Albert Evans, 'Michael Howard is "not sure" if he was right to sack Boris Johnson for lying when he was Tory leader', *i*, 11 July 2019, https://inews.co.uk/news/politics/michael-howard-boris-johnson-sacked-tory-leadership-election-latest-news-312600.)

§ Gaby Hinsliff, 'Boris Johnson sacked by Tories over private life',

The Guardian's verdict, while understandable, was premature. Fifteen years later Boris Johnson, who'd been sacked for lying both by *The Times* and by the Tory Party, became prime minister. He had been elected by a majority of Tory MPs – and was powerfully endorsed by *The Times*.*

JOHNSON'S DEBT TO HUNTER S. THOMPSON

The transgressive discourse I explored in the paragraphs above can be traced to the so-called New Journalism of the 1960s and 1970s, in which writers such as Truman Capote, Norman Mailer and Tom Wolfe deliberately blurred the boundaries between reporting and fiction. The New Journalism was especially stimulated by the 'gonzo journalism' of Hunter S. Thompson's *Fear and Loathing in Las Vegas* (1972), which was written entirely in the first person and highlighted interior experience to the exclusion of everything else.

In theory an account of a convention in Las Vegas, it

The Guardian, 14 November 2004, https://www.theguardian.com/politics/2004/nov/14/uk.conservatives.

* *The Times* endorsed Boris Johnson in both the leadership election of July 2019 and the general election in December ('The Times view on the next prime minister: Boris Johnson at No 10', *The Times*, 6 July 2019, https://www.thetimes.co.uk/article/the-times-view-on-the-next-prime-minister-boris-johnson-at-no-10-njpzrff8v; 'The Times's endorsement for the general election: Back to the Future', *The Times*, 11 December 2019, https://www.thetimes.co.uk/article/the-times-s-endorsement-for-the-general-election-back-to-the-future-bmtz9gv97).

focused on the adventures of a drug-crazed reporter sent to cover it. Mailer's *Miami and the Siege of Chicago* (1968) is an earlier and more brilliant example. This writer-foregrounding reportage works because these writers were better stylists than their followers. They were also in their way writing truthfully about their responses to events, while making these subjective responses the story rather than the events.

Furthermore, *Fear and Loathing* had a moral premise of sorts: the conference and American society were themselves so crazy that they made sense only to a hallucinating observer. Thompson wrote that 'fiction is a bridge to the truth that the mechanics of journalism can't reach', adding that 'you have to add up the facts in your own fuzzy way'.* Their techniques were copied, though without conviction, in Britain. In the 1980s, one famous journalist would attend party conferences where, colleagues recall, they would establish themselves with large quantities of drugs and alcohol in their hotel room to watch the coverage on television, thus foregrounding the experience of the reporter and converting politics into background.†

It was Boris Johnson who possessed the confidence and

---

* Dick Polman, 'A new book describes Hunter S. Thompson's prescience', *The Atlantic*, 28 December 2018, https://www.theatlantic.com/politics/archive/2018/12/hunter-s-thompsons-writing-foreshadowed-rise-trump/578395.

† Will Self followed suit, taking heroin in the prime minister's plane while following John Major in the 1997 general election.

creative genius to inject gonzo journalism into mainstream British political reporting. He landed in Brussels thirty years ago in the same spirit as Hunter S. Thompson in Las Vegas, though without the drugs. At the heart of his reporting was Thompson's insight that fiction and fact could merge.

By some margin the most brilliant political journalist of his generation, with a talent that at times crossed over the line to genius, Johnson infuriated rivals but created a new school of reporting. He reinvented political language and discourse, rustling up new phrases in the same way that a Michelin-starred chef produces dishes, and in the process changed the nature not just of journalism but in due course of British public life. Johnson was capable within a few paragraphs of invoking P. G. Wodehouse, Greek tragedy, a sophisticated take on the latest ideas on public sector reform and a crude sexual joke. But at the heart of his reporting work was a repudiation of the ethics that until then had defined journalist values at Westminster: fairness, accuracy, scruple, scepticism, fact checking.

Johnson's achievement cannot be explained simply in terms of journalistic fashion. In his famous essay on politics and the English language, George Orwell observed that 'the decline of a language must ultimately have political and economic causes: it is not due simply to the bad influence of this or that individual writer'.* The solipsism which lay

---

* George Orwell, 'Politics and the English Language', in *Shooting an Elephant and Other Essays* (London: Secker & Warburg, 1950).

at the heart of Johnson's prose was a consequence of a social and economic shift that transformed Britain over the last fifty years. In the aftermath of the Second World War, identities were collective: regiment; trade union; community; church; country; family; political party. The most admired qualities were duty, courage, self-sacrifice – all of which required individuals to submerge their personalities in the interests of an institution or the nation.

Johnson abandoned all of these for a narcissism that mocked the style of straightforward, sober, serious, self-effacing politics of the post-war era. He turned his back on the public domain and the ideas of duty, honour and obligation that defined it. For him, politics was a personal story which saw the evolution of Britain's first gonzo political journalist into our first gonzo prime minister. The parallels with Donald Trump are instructive.

Boris Johnson's and Donald Trump's Rise to Power: a Comparison

During Donald Trump's 2016 presidential campaign, he made much of his career as a real estate tycoon and hotel magnate.* He told how he started in business with a

---

* Eli Stokols, 'Trump tries to sell himself as the comeback kid', *Politico*, 3 October 2016, https://www.politico.com/story/2016/10/donald-trump-colorado-comeback-229070. This strategy worked: see 'Why they love Trump: "He's a successful businessman"', BBC News, 10 June 2016, https://www.bbc.co.uk/news/av/election-us-2016-36495727.

$1 million loan from his father and turned it into a $10 billion fortune before moving into politics.*

The truth was more complicated. Trump actually inherited tens of millions from his father, who also bailed him out when he got into trouble.† The idea that he made $10 billion during a business career which started in 1968 when he went to work at his father Fred's real estate development company, E. Trump & Son, and ended in multiple bankruptcies in the 1990s is almost certain to be false.‡

Trump himself, in one of the moments of candour which at times makes it possible to like him, was straightforward about this talent for stretching the truth in his best-selling book, *The Art of the Deal*. He hailed a quality which he called 'truthful hyperbole' which, said Trump, 'plays to

---

* Scott Stump, 'Donald Trump: My dad gave me "a small loan" of $1 million to get started', CNBC, 26 October 2015, https://www.cnbc.com/2015/10/26/donald-trump-my-dad-gave-me-a-small-loan-of-1-million-to-get-started.html.

† Glenn Kessler, 'Trump's false claim he built his empire with a "small loan" from his father', *Washington Post*, 3 March 2016, https://www.washingtonpost.com/news/fact-checker/wp/2016/03/03/trumps-false-claim-he-built-his-empire-with-a-small-loan-from-his-father/.

‡ Ana Swanson, 'The myth and the reality of Donald Trump's business empire', *Washington Post*, 29 February 2016, https://www.washingtonpost.com/news/wonk/wp/2016/02/29/the-myth-and-the-reality-of-donald-trumps-business-empire/.

people's fantasies'.* Trump calls this technique of selling real estate 'an innocent form of exaggeration'.

In the early years of the twenty-first century Donald Trump was in financial trouble, and in 2004 Trump Hotels and Casinos filed for bankruptcy.† His redemption came thanks to *The Apprentice*, a reality TV show in which he played the role of a powerful chief executive while contestants competed to work at the Trump Corporation. At the end of each episode, Trump disposed of contestants by pointing a finger at the loser with the trademark catchphrase: 'You're fired.' The show enabled him to present himself to a national audience as a successful businessman, even though some banks had pulled the plug on him.

It is reasonable to assert that it was his reincarnation as a reality TV star, not that dubious fortune in real estate, which gave Trump the launching pad to make a run for the White House. Like Johnson, he was an exotic creation of celebrity media culture. Like so many other celebrities, he invited his audience lose themselves in a fantasy world created by him, in which he alone defined success and failure, truth and falsehood.

---

* Carlos Lozada, 'How Donald Trump plays the press, in his own words', *Washington Post*, 17 June 2015, https://www.washingtonpost.com/news/book-party/wp/2015/06/17/how-donald-trump-plays-the-press-in-his-own-words/.

† Russ Buettner and Charles V. Bagli, 'How Donald Trump bankrupted his Atlantic City casinos, but still earned millions', *New York Times*, 12 June 2016, https://www.nytimes.com/2016/06/12/nyregion/donald-trump-atlantic-city.html.

Britain and America carried out a joint experiment. Truth-twisting techniques drawn from show business, which proved stunningly successful in marketing political campaigns, are now becoming part of government. In the next chapter I will examine how Donald Trump and Boris Johnson have performed once in power rather than on the campaign trail, starting with their handling of coronavirus. The coronavirus pandemic is the most tragic example of why techniques drawn from show business, though they can be an effective campaigning tool, do not work in government.

Chapter Five

THE CANDOUR OF ANGELA MERKEL

'The pandemic cannot be fought with lies and disinformation, and neither can it be with hatred and agitation. Fact-denying populism is being shown its limits. In a democracy, facts and transparency are needed.'

ANGELA MERKEL, EUROPEAN PARLIAMENT, BRUSSELS,
8 JULY 2020

In the last chapter I examined the talent of Boris Johnson and Donald Trump as gifted popular entertainers who had transferred to politics. Neither the prime minister nor the president possessed the moral seriousness to cope with a public health catastrophe like coronavirus. Neither leader was able to find the right language to talk about a disease which claimed the lives of tens of thousands of their fellow citizens. Indeed, both men were slow to grasp that a problem existed at all. As a result they were too late to take action. When people started to die in large numbers, both the US president and the British prime minister responded with lies and fabrications.

Donald Trump's conduct was grotesque. At least Boris Johnson did not refer to coronavirus as a 'hoax',* invite people to inject themselves with bleach† or promote an anti-malarial drug which increased risk of death when used to treat coronavirus patients.‡ But Johnson and his ministers certainly did systematically mislead voters, repeatedly boast about imaginary achievements, and exploit the Tory government's phalanx of press support to shift the blame,§

---

* Lauren Egan, 'Trump calls coronavirus Democrats' "new hoax"', NBC News, 29 February 2020, https://www.nbcnews.com/politics/donald-trump/trump-calls-coronavirus-democrats-new-hoax-n1145721.

† 'Coronavirus: Outcry after Trump suggests injecting disinfectant as treatment', BBC News, 24 April 2020, https://www.bbc.co.uk/news/world-us-canada-52407177.

‡ Ariana Eunjung Cha and Laurie McGinley, 'Antimalarial drug touted by President Trump is linked to increased risk of death in coronavirus patients, study says', *Washington Post*, 22 May 2020, https://www.washingtonpost.com/health/2020/05/22/hydroxychloroquine-coronavirus-study/.

§ An example came with the consistent hostile briefing against civil servants at the height of the coronavirus pandemic. A case in point came from the political editor of *The Spectator*, James Forsyth, in an article entitled 'The British state needs rewiring'. Forsyth expounds the limitations of Public Health England and quotes a number of unnamed sources including one 'Whitehall veteran' who claims the ten days leading up to 23 March were 'the nearest the wiring of the state has come to collapse. It wasn't just blowing a fuse: the motherboard was beginning to melt down.' James Forsyth, 'The British state needs rewiring', *The Spectator*, 16 May 2020, https://www.spectator.co.uk/article/the-british-state-needs-rewiring.

rather than owning up to errors which cost the lives of thousands.

Most of the lies, falsehoods and misleading statements made by Johnson and his ministers about coronavirus are not included in this chapter. There are too many to deal with. They involved all aspects of the government response, from bogus schemes procuring protective equipment to dishonest support of Johnson's adviser Dominic Cummings after he flouted lockdown rules. Almost every day produced new examples, and I hope to publish them all separately.* For the time being I will concentrate on the culture of deceit and exaggeration at the top of the British and American governments as coronavirus raged.

EARLY RESPONSES TO THE PANDEMIC

Barely a month before the pandemic started, Johns Hopkins University published a study of global readiness to deal with health emergencies, for example speed of response and how well health services would 'treat the sick and protect health workers'.† The report could not have been more timely. The academics‡ ranked 195 nations according to their

---

* See https://boris-johnson-lies.com/.

† *Global Health Security Index 2019: Building Collective Action and Accountability*, Nuclear Threat Initiative, October 2019, https://www. ghsindex.org/wp-content/uploads/2019/10/2019-Global-Health-Security-Index.pdf, p. 8.

‡ The *GHS Index* is a project of the Nuclear Threat Initiative and the

ability to cope. Their study warned that 'no country is fully prepared for epidemics or pandemics, and every country has important gaps to address'. It went on to rank the United States and the United Kingdom as the two countries in the best position to handle a pandemic.

There were good reasons to think those judgements were sensible. The United States and Britain are advanced nations with decent infrastructure, famed scientific expertise and financial muscle. Britain has a famous National Health Service which is available to all citizens. Yet the Johns Hopkins experts were wrong in their predictions. Britain and the United States have been two of the worst-performing countries in the world.

By October, more than 32 million people had been infected, with a million dead.* Almost 42,000 of these deaths (around 4 per cent of the total) were British.† Britain's excess death tally per capita was the highest in Europe.‡ It suffered more deaths than any European

---

Johns Hopkins Center for Health Security and was developed with the Economist Intelligence Unit. Ibid., p. 5. David Milliken and William Schomberg, 'UK GDP collapsed nearly 20% in second quarter in historic COVID hit', *Reuters*, 30 September 2020, https://uk.reuters.com/article/us-britain-economy/uk-gdp-collapsed-nearly-20-in-second-quarter-in-historic-covid-hit-idUKKBN26L0SB.

* https://www.bbc.co.uk/news/world-54334496.

† 'Coronavirus (COVID-19) in the UK', Gov.uk, https://coronavirus.data.gov.uk/

‡ 'Adam Vaugan, 'England & Wales had most excess deaths in Europe's Covid-19 first wave', *New Scientist*, 14 October 2020, https://www.newscientist.com/article/2256986-england-

country and had the third highest mortality rate per head.

The US was the worst-hit nation with close to 200,000 deaths and a mortality rate just lower than Britain's. It was said by experts at the start of the crisis that governments had to choose between inflicting damage on the economy or saving lives. In fact, Johnson's Britain and Trump's America performed dreadfully on both fronts. Not only was Britain one of the worst nations for deaths per head, it also suffered a far worse recession than the US or the Eurozone – its GDP was shown to have fallen more than 20 per cent between April and June.[*]

This demands explanation. It was not just that the experts failed to foresee the disasters in the UK and the US. They also failed to predict that other countries – for example New Zealand, South Korea and Germany, ranked fourteenth to Britain's second – would perform far better.

At the heart of Johns Hopkins's miscalculation was a failure to take into account political leadership.[†] Speaking to

---

wales-had-most-excess-deaths-in-europes-covid-19-first-wave/.

[*] Andrew Walker, 'Coronavirus: UK economy could be among worst hit of leading nations, says OECD', BBC News, 10 June 2020, https://www.bbc.co.uk/news/business-52991913.

[†] For a good account of British failures see (1) Jonathan Calvert, George Arbuthnott and Jonathan Leake, 'Coronavirus: 38 days when Britain sleepwalked into disaster', *Sunday Times*, 19 April 2020, www.thetimes.co.uk/article/coronavirus-38-days-when-britain-

the European Parliament as Germany took over the presidency of the European Commission in July 2020, German chancellor Angela Merkel told MEPs: 'The pandemic can't be fought with lies and disinformation, and neither can it be with hatred and agitation. Fact-denying populism is being shown its limits. In a democracy, facts and transparency are needed.'[*]

By July it was becoming obvious that Merkel's Germany had emerged in better shape from the coronavirus pandemic than Trump's America and Johnson's United Kingdom. There are many reasons for this, and it is too soon to reach anything like the definitive answer. Many different factors applied, from demography to proximity to transport hubs (which may explain why cities such as New York and London fared especially badly, and why eastern Europe escaped better than western Europe). But it is certainly not premature to note the difference between the careful response of leaders like Angela Merkel in Germany,

---

sleepwalked-into-disaster-hq3b9tlgh; (2) Toby Helm, Emma Graham-Harrison and Robin McKie, 'How did Britain get its coronavirus response so wrong?', *The Guardian*, 19 April 2020, https://www.theguardian.com/world/2020/apr/18/how-did-britain-get-its-response-to-coronavirus-so-wrong; (3) David Conn et al., 'Revealed: the inside story of the UK's Covid-19 crisis', *The Guardian*, 29 April 2020, https://www.theguardian.com/world/2020/apr/29/revealed-the-inside-story-of-uk-covid-19-coronavirus-crisis.

[*] John Daniszewski, 'In struggle against pandemic, populist leaders fare poorly', AP, 23 July 2020, https://apnews.com/2a4b5159e9c8b1510973801297243c3d.

Moon Jae-in in South Korea and Jacinda Ardern in New Zealand, and the response of Donald Trump and Boris Johnson.*

Angela Merkel and Boris Johnson: A Study in Contrast

Perhaps New Zealand, with its small, isolated population in a remote part of the world, counts as a special case. The same cannot be said of Germany, which was confronted with its first cases of the pandemic at almost exactly the same time as Britain. Both countries considered themselves to be relatively well prepared,† and both at first

---

* Other leaders accused of covering up issues in their response to Covid-19 include Xi Jinping in China, Vladimir Putin in Russia and Jair Bolsonaro in Brazil. Tom Mitchell, 'What Xi knew: pressure builds on China's leader', *Financial Times*, 21 May 2020, https://www.ft.com/content/3a294233-6983-428c-b74b-3cc58c713eb8; 'Russia's covid-19 outbreak is far worse than the Kremlin admits', *The Economist*, 21 May 2020, https://www.economist.com/europe/2020/05/21/russias-covid-19-outbreak-is-far-worse-than-the-kremlin-admits; Tom Phillips and Caio Barretto Briso, 'Judge orders Bolsonaro to resume publishing Brazil Covid-19 data', *The Guardian*, 9 June 2020, https://www.theguardian.com/world/2020/jun/09/judge-orders-bolsonaro-to-resume-publishing-brazil-covid-19-data.

† UK: 'Matt Hancock MP makes statement on Wuhan coronavirus', UK Parliament, 23 January 2020, https://www.parliament.uk/business/news/2020/january/statement-on-wuhan-coronavirus/; Germany: Sylvia Cunningham, 'Jens Spahn says coronavirus has arrived as epidemic in Europe, Germany is well-prepared', KCRW Berlin, 25 February 2020, https://kcrwberlin.com/2020/02/in-brief-jens-spahn-says-coronavirus-has-arrived-as-epidemic-in-europe-germany-is-well-prepared/.

underestimated the danger. Germany, with a population slightly larger than Britain,* ended up (at the time of writing) with better outcomes.

Right from the start, Germany took the World Health Organization (WHO) advice, issued on 23 January, that the world should prepare 'for containment, including active surveillance, early detection, isolation and case management, contact tracing and prevention of onward spread'.† Germany was lucky. Even before the WHO concluded that coronavirus could be transmitted from one human to another, German scientists had created a reliable test which detected the virus.‡

By contrast, the UK was slow to start testing. At the start of the pandemic, the UK did attempt to trace early cases.

---

* UK population is estimated to be around 67 million ('Population estimates', Office for National Statistics, 24 June 2020, https://www.ons.gov.uk/peoplepopulationandcommunity/ populationandmigration/populationestimates). German population is estimated to be around 84 million ('Germany population', Worldometer, https://www.worldometers.info/world-population/ germany-population/).

† 'Statement on the first meeting of the International Health Regulations (2005) Emergency Committee regarding the outbreak of novel coronavirus (2019-nCoV)', World Health Organization, 23 January 2020, https://www.who.int/news-room/ detail/23-01-2020-statement-on-the-meeting-of-the-international- health-regulations-(2005)-emergency-committee-regarding-the- outbreak-of-novel-coronavirus-(2019-ncov).

‡ Constantin Eckner, 'How Germany has managed to perform so many Covid-19 tests', *The Spectator*, 6 April 2020, https://www.spectator.co.uk/ article/how-germany-has-managed-to-perform-so-many-covid-19-tests.

However, this did not continue beyond 12 March, when Boris Johnson announced that anyone with symptoms must stay at home for seven days.* As the Royal Society of Medicine's Gabriel Scally later said: 'Abandoning testing gave the virus the green light to spread uncontrollably.'†

The decision to abandon contact tracing was in defiance of guidance from the WHO.

Prime Minister Johnson failed for a long time to grasp the significance of the crisis. He was not paying attention.

---

* According to the government's testing chief, Professor John Newton, this was in response to forecasting that the UK could soon face 1 million cases, far too many for the track and trace system in place at the time. 'At that point, the Government made the decision to move to lockdown as the most appropriate response to the epidemiology in the UK at the time,' Professor Newton told the Science and Technology Select Committee in May 2020. See Alain Tolhurst, 'Coronavirus: UK's testing chief says track and trace was ditched in March due to forecast of one million cases', PoliticsHome, 22 May 2020, https://www.politicshome.com/news/article/coronavirus-uks-testing-chief-says-track-and-trace-was-abandoned-in-march-due-to-forecast-of-a-million-cases; 'Prime Minister's statement on coronavirus (COVID-19): 12 March 2020', Gov.uk, https://www.gov.uk/government/speeches/pm-statement-on-coronavirus-12-march-2020; 'Coronavirus: Track and trace system in place from June – PM', BBC News, 20 May 2020, https://www.bbc.co.uk/news/uk-52741331; letter from Greg Clark, chair, Science and Technology Select Committee, to Boris Johnson, 18 May 2020, https://publications.parliament.uk/pa/cm5801/cmselect/cmsctech/correspondence/200518-Chair-to-Prime-Minister-re-COVID-19-pandemic-some-lessons-learned-so-far.pdf.

† Luke McGee and Mick Krever, 'Where did it go wrong for the UK on coronavirus?', CNN, 1 May 2020, https://edition.cnn.com/2020/04/30/uk/britain-coronavirus-missteps-boris-johnson-analysis-gbr-intl/index.html.

During the early weeks, when the crucial decisions were being made, Johnson retreated to the country for a 'working holiday'.* A *Sunday Times* article highlighted that Johnson 'skipped five Cobra meetings on the virus' and did not attend one until 2 March, five weeks after the first took place.† As late as 5 March, Johnson said: 'As far as possible, it should be business as usual for the overwhelming majority of people in this country.'‡ This last remark was made five weeks after the WHO had announced that Covid-19 was a public health emergency of international concern and six

---

* Calvert, Arbuthnott and Leake, 'Coronavirus: 38 days when Britain sleepwalked into disaster'.

† Ibid. COBRA is the civil contingencies committee convened to handle matters of national emergency. Meetings can only be attended by civil servants, and chaired by ministers. Speaking on Sky News, Michael Gove said: 'The idea that the prime minister skipped meetings that were vital to our response to the coronavirus, I think, is grotesque.' He told Andrew Marr: 'Most COBRA meetings don't have the prime minister attending them. That is the whole point.' He argued COBRA meetings were 'led by the relevant secretary of state in the relevant area'. But Damian McBride, former adviser to Gordon Brown, tweeted: 'During the Foot & Mouth crisis in 2007, GB didn't just attend every COBRA meeting, he chaired them all. There were no "experts" telling him when to tune in. If that's what we got from a PM for a disease that didn't even threaten human life, was it too much to ask for coronavirus?' Damian McBride (@DPMcBride), Twitter, 19 April 2020, https://twitter.com/dpmcbride/status/1251863181980512257?lang=en.

‡ 'Boris Johnson and Chris Whitty, chief medical officer, on coronavirus – summary and analysis', *The Guardian*, 5 March 2020, https://www.theguardian.com/politics/live/2020/mar/05/chief-medical-officer-chris-whitty-questioned-by-mps-live-news?page=with:block-5e60df108f08c2df6d273b17#block-5e60df108f08c2df6d273b17.

days before it declared it a pandemic.* By this stage, schools were being closed in parts of Germany.†

With Germany (and most of Europe) locking down, Johnson was effectively in denial. Though advised not to shake hands, he boasted he 'shook hands with everybody' on a visit to a hospital.‡ In mid-March the UK allowed the Cheltenham Festival, with crowds of around 150,000, to go ahead.§ A week earlier, Johnson attended a Six Nations rugby match at Twickenham.¶

This sense of personal impunity probably explains why Johnson (along with some of his ministers and officials) fell ill with the disease. From the end of March until the

---

* 'Timeline of WHO's response to COVID-19', World Health Organization, 29 June 2020, https://www.who.int/news-room/detail/29-06-2020-covidtimeline.

† 'Sechs Coronavirus-Fälle in NRW – Karneval sorgt für "neue Qualität"', RP Online, 27 February 2020, https://rp-online.de/nrw/staedte/duesseldorf/coronavirus-in-nrw-sechs-coronavirus-faelle-in-nrw-karneval-und-kitas-im-fokus_aid-49191227.

‡ Rowena Mason, 'Boris Johnson boasted of shaking hands on day Sage warned not to', *The Guardian*, 5 May 2020, https://www.theguardian.com/politics/2020/may/05/boris-johnson-boasted-of-shaking-hands-on-day-sage-warned-not-to.

§ Hayley Mortimer, 'Coronavirus: Cheltenham Festival "may have accelerated" spread', BBC News, 30 April 2020, https://www.bbc.co.uk/news/uk-england-gloucestershire-52485584.

¶ James Wood, 'Boris Johnson and fiancee Carrie Symonds are spotted in public for first time since announcing they were expecting a baby as they watch England beat Wales 33-30 at Twickenham', *MailOnline*, 7 March 2020, https://www.dailymail.co.uk/news/article-8086403/Boris-Johnson-fiancee-Carrie-Symonds-spotted-watching-England-play-rugby-against-Wales.html.

middle of April, the prime minister was either self-isolating in Downing Street or in hospital in intensive care.* By the time he had re-emerged, it was clear for everyone to see that the British government had made serious errors in the early handling of the virus. This phase of the crisis brings me to the second area of contrast between Johnson and Merkel. With events moving against them, Johnson and his ministers resorted to a series of falsehoods.

WHY MANY FEWER GERMANS DIED

Throughout the coronavirus crisis, Angela Merkel was straight with the German people. She was calm, pragmatic and open. The writer Saskia Miller interviewed Axel Radlach Pries, from the Berlin Institute of Health, about Merkel's leadership during the crisis. Her account is thought-provoking:

> When I spoke with him, Pries stressed the significance of receiving honest communication from the highest levels of leadership during the outbreak. Merkel has relied heavily, and very publicly, on the expertise of a handful of experts,

---

* On 27 March Johnson tested positive. By 6 April he had been rushed to intensive care in hospital where he remained until 9 April. He was discharged on 12 April and finally returned to Downing Street and work on 27 April. See 'PM's Covid-19 timeline: from "mild symptoms" to a brush with death', https://www.theguardian.com/world/2020/apr/05/timeline-boris-johnson-and-coronavirus.

including the now famous Christian Drosten,* the head of virology at the Charité hospital in Berlin. From the perspective of the public, Pries said, the chancellor and the virologist 'are very trustworthy'. People know 'that what they get from both Drosten and Angela Merkel are real and very well-considered facts' and that the two also 'share information about what they *don't* know'. Because they are 'honest with respect to their information', he said, that information is seen as credible. This honesty, at a time of widespread disinformation, Pries told me, was playing a big role in persuading Germans largely to continue to follow the rules and maintain, even now, 'a very calm situation in Germany'.†

Miller carried out this interview with Pries in mid-April. By now, the signs were that Germany was coming through the pandemic relatively well. On 17 April, authorities

---

* Drosten is one of the world's leading experts on coronaviruses, and, back in 2003, he and a colleague were the first Western scientists to discover SARS after China hid information about that outbreak. Rob Schmitz, '"Das Coronavirus" podcast captivates Germany with scientific info on the pandemic', NPR, 31 March 2020, https://www.npr.org/2020/03/31/823865329/das-coronavirus-podcast-captivates-germany-with-scientific-info-on-the-pandemic.

† Saskia Miller, 'The secret to Germany's COVID-19 success: Angela Merkel is a scientist', *The Atlantic*, 20 April 2020, https://www.theatlantic.com/international/archive/2020/04/angela-merkel-germany-coronavirus-pandemic/610225/.

announced that the pandemic was under control.* They had suffered 3,868 deaths out of an 84 million population, compared to Britain's 14,576 from 67 million.† It is excruciating and a matter of deep national embarrassment to compare Angela Merkel's good sense with never-ending iterations of bombast, exaggeration and falsehood from Boris Johnson once he had returned to work towards the end of April.

Johnson claimed from the steps of Downing Street that 'I know there will be many people looking at our apparent success'.‡ This was bizarre. Britain's death toll had already reached 20,000. Just over a week later, on 5 May, the UK became the nation with the highest number of deaths in Europe and the second globally, behind the US.§

At this point the government entered the realm of fantasy. On 1 May Johnson and his health secretary claimed that Britain had met its target of 100,000 daily coronavirus

---

* 'Coronavirus: Germany says its outbreak is "under control"', BBC News, 17 April 2020, https://www.bbc.co.uk/news/world-europe-52327956.

† 'As it happened: Trump says lockdown protesters being treated "rough"', BBC News, 17 April 2020, https://www.bbc.co.uk/news/live/world-52319956.

‡ Gareth Davies, 'Boris Johnson's coronavirus speech in full', *The Telegraph*, 27 April 2020, https://www.telegraph.co.uk/politics/2020/04/27/boris-johnsons-coronavirus-speech-full/.

§ 'Coronavirus: UK death toll passes Italy to be highest in Europe', BBC News, 5 May 2020, https://www.bbc.co.uk/news/uk-52549860.

tests.* This was a fabrication.† For weeks that followed, Johnson and his ministerial team would continue to make false claims about Britain's record on testing.‡

The issue got so bad that Chris Hopson, chief executive of NHS Providers – the membership organisation for all of England's 217 ambulance, community, hospital and mental health trusts – told Johnson to stop the rhetoric. On 7 June, Hopson said: 'The real concern is that we don't have that same degree of trust, because we're not having the kind of honest and open debates that we need. We seem to be resorting to kind of fairly cheap political rhetoric about stuff being world-class, when it clearly isn't.'§

---

* UK Prime Minister (@10Downing Street), 'On 30 April there were 122,347 #coronavirus tests, exceeding our target of 100,000 tests per day', Twitter, 2 May 2020, https://twitter.com/10DowningStreet/status/1256499898075230210; 'Coronavirus: Target reached as UK tests pass 100,000 a day', BBC News, 1 May 2020, https://www.bbc.co.uk/news/uk-52508836.

† 'Has the government really hit 100,000 tests a day, and what happens next?', Full Fact, 1 May 2020, https://fullfact.org/health/coronavirus-100k-tests/.

‡ Matt Hancock (@MattHancock), 'Great that we have hit 100k tests for a second day running – now our large testing capacity is up and running', Twitter, 2 May 2020, https://twitter.com/MattHancock/status/1256607298555912192; Hansard, HC Deb, 6 May 2020, vol. 675, col. 549.

§ Kate Forrester, 'PM urged to "ditch political rhetoric" amid fears of coronavirus second wave – as Keir Starmer narrows gap in polls', PoliticsHome, 7 June 2020, https://www.politicshome.com/news/article/pm-urged-to-ditch-political-rhetoric-amid-fears-of-coronavirus-second-wave-as-keir-starmer-narrows-gap-in-polls.

Again and again experts contradicted Johnson's and Hancock's claims. The chair of the UK Statistics Authority, Sir David Norgrove, wrote a withering letter to the health secretary saying: 'The aim seems to be to show the largest possible number of tests, even at the expense of understanding.' He added: 'It is not surprising that, given their inadequacy, data on testing are so widely criticised and often mistrusted.'*

Throughout the crisis, government ministers insisted that the UK's response had been without fault. A mantra developed: government had 'taken the right steps at the right time'. Matt Hancock told the *Today* programme on 11 April: 'We took the right measures at the right time.'†
In the daily press briefing on 17 April, Business Secretary Alok Sharma said: 'At each point we have been following scientific and medical advice and we have been deliberate in our actions – taking the right steps at the right time.'‡ Then again on 22 April, Dominic Raab parroted the phrase when

---

* 'Sir David Norgrove response to Matt Hancock regarding the Government's COVID-19 testing data', UK Statistics Authority, 2 June 2020, https://uksa.statisticsauthority.gov.uk/correspondence/sir-david-norgrove-response-to-matt-hancock-regarding-the-governments-covid-19-testing-data/.

† Claire Anderson, 'Hancock torn apart for saying UK has bigger population than Italy as he defends death toll', *Express*, 11 April 2020, https://www.express.co.uk/news/uk/1267804/matt-hancock-coronavirus-uk-latest-radio-4-today-italy-death-toll-covid-19-update.

‡ 'Business Secretary's statement on coronavirus (COVID-19): 17 April 2020', Gov.uk, https://www.gov.uk/government/speeches/business-secretarys-statement-on-coronavirus-covid-19-17-april-2020.

he told another briefing that 'we have been deliberate in our actions so that we take the right steps at the right time'.*

This was nonsense. The government was slow to stop public events, ditched the test and trace strategy early only to return to it later, wasted time with a dangerous herd immunity strategy, missed the deadline for a joint EU ventilator procurement scheme,† failed to

---

* 'Foreign Secretary's statement on coronavirus (COVID-19): 22 April 2020', Gov.uk, https://www.gov.uk/government/speeches/foreign-secretarys-statement-on-coronavirus-covid-19-22-april-2020.

† 'Coronavirus: "Mix-up" over EU ventilator scheme', BBC News, 26 March 2020, https://www.bbc.co.uk/news/uk-politics-52052694. When the government missed out on joining an EU scheme to procure ventilators, it claimed it had missed the deadline after not being sent the relevant emails. Comments made by Matt Hancock on BBC *Question Time* a week earlier soon began to circulate. They appeared to show he was aware of the scheme. When asked about the scheme where twenty-five EU countries were coming together to buy ventilators, the health secretary said: 'We are invited to be part of that.' (Sarah Mackie (@lumi_1984), 'Matt Hancock last week on Question Time: "...we are invited to be part of that...we engaged with that process today"', Twitter, 26 March 2020, https://twitter.com/lumi_1984/status/1243240883455234049.) On 30 March, *The Guardian* reported that it had seen EU minutes showing that 'a British official had joined eight out of twelve EU health security committee meetings dedicated to the Covid-19 outbreak since the group was set up earlier this year, shortly before China's Hubei province was put into lockdown' (Jennifer Rankin, 'UK discussed joint EU plan to buy Covid-19 medical supplies, say officials', *The Guardian*, 30 March 2020, https://www.theguardian.com/world/2020/mar/30/uk-discussed-joint-eu-plan-to-buy-covid-19-medical-supplies-say-officials). According to the minutes, at least four of those meetings discussed EU procurement schemes. On 21 April, the government was further embarrassed when Simon McDonald, the top civil

introduce its track and trace app on time. The list could go on.

LYING ABOUT CARE HOMES

And some of the lies told by the government were very dark. Take the statements about care homes made by the prime minister and his health secretary, Matt Hancock.

By the first week of June, official figures showed more than 16,000 residents of British care and nursing homes had died.[*] Johnson's determination to shield hospitals and protect the NHS had left residents of care homes and staff vulnerable. The death toll was far worse than in other countries. Just 3,000 had died in Germany, where no one was allowed into care homes from hospitals without a negative Covid-19 test, and none at all in Hong Kong, where care homes were in lockdown.[†]

---

servant at the Foreign Office, told the Commons Foreign Affairs Committee that ministers took a 'political decision' not to join an EU drive to procure ventilators and protective equipment. He retracted his statement later that day (George Parker, Helen Warrell and Laura Pitel, 'UK ministers struggle for control of coronavirus strategy', *Financial Times*, 22 April 2020, https://www.ft.com/content/a265fac3-b659-4fbc-b07d-769d281fa42f).

[*] Robert Booth and Pamela Duncan, 'More than 16,000 people in UK care homes have died from coronavirus', *The Guardian*, 16 June 2020, https://www.theguardian.com/world/2020/jun/16/more-than-16000-people-in-uk-care-homes-have-died-from-coronavirus.

[†] Robert Booth, 'MPs hear why Hong Kong had no Covid-19 care home deaths', *The Guardian*, 19 May 2020, https://www.theguardian.com/world/2020/may/19/

Meanwhile in Britain many patients were discharged from hospital and sent to homes for the elderly and vulnerable without being tested.* There is also plenty of testimony that the government failed to provide adequate protective equipment. So it was no surprise when newly elected Labour leader Keir Starmer raised the issue of government guidance for care homes in the Commons. He said: 'Earlier this year, and until 12 March, the government's own official advice was, and I'm quoting from it, "it remains very unlikely that people receiving care in a care home will become infected".'†

Johnson immediately responded: 'It wasn't true that the advice said that.'‡ Johnson was wrong. The guidance

---

mps-hear-why-hong-kong-had-no-covid-19-care-home-deaths; Robert Booth, 'Covid-19: risk of death in UK care homes 13 times higher than in Germany', *The Guardian*, 28 June 2020, https://www.theguardian.com/world/2020/jun/28/covid-19-risk-of-death-in-uk-care-homes-13-times-higher-than-in-germany; Andrew MacAskill and Stephen Grey, 'Exclusive: Review contradicts Boris Johnson on claims he ordered early lockdown at UK care homes', Reuters, 15 May 2020, https://www.reuters.com/article/us-health-coronavirus-britain-carehomes/exclusive-review-contradicts-boris-johnson-on-claims-he-ordered-early-lockdown-at-uk-care-homes-idUSKBN22R1O2. By the end of June, care home deaths from Covid-19 had risen to 19,394.

* Guidelines said there was no need to test discharged patients because Covid-19 sufferers 'can be safely cared for in a care home'; see Robert Booth, 'Why did so many people die of Covid-19 in the UK's care homes?', *The Guardian*, 28 May 2020, https://www.theguardian.com/society/2020/may/28/why-did-so-many-people-die-of-covid-19-in-the-uks-care-homes.

† Hansard, HC Deb, 13 May 2020, vol. 676, col. 240.

‡ Ibid.

published on 25 February states that it was 'very unlikely' people receiving care in care homes or the community would be infected with the new coronavirus.* This advice was withdrawn on 13 March and replaced with new guidance about what to do in the event of an outbreak at a care home or other supported living.† Starmer has since asked Johnson to return to the House to correct the record. The prime minister has failed to do so.

Johnson claimed in the same PMQs that 'we brought in the lockdown in care homes ahead of the general lockdown'.‡ The prime minister's spokesman told reporters later that day that Johnson had been referring to government advice to care homes, issued on 13 March. This advice, he said, was 'recommending essential visits only, that obviously came before we took steps nationwide in relation to social distancing'.§ However, a Reuters investigation which reviewed the guidance and spoke to three care home providers found 'no evidence that any such early lockdown was ordered'.¶

---

* Booth, 'Why did so many people die of Covid-19 in the UK's care homes?'

† 'COVID-19: guidance for supported living and home care', Gov. uk, 13 March 2020, https://www.gov.uk/government/publications/covid-19-residential-care-supported-living-and-home-care-guidance.

‡ Hansard, HC Deb, 13 May 2020, vol. 676, col. 240.

§ MacAskill and Grey, 'Exclusive: Review contradicts Boris Johnson on claims he ordered early lockdown at UK care homes'.

¶ Ibid.

Joyce Pinfield, who is in charge of running two care homes and sits on the board of directors at the National Care Association, said, 'The guidance should have been far better. It was left to care providers to make their own decisions.'* Julie Nicholls, manager of the Appleby Lodge residential home in Cornwall, said that she 'definitely didn't have any government guidance' and that 'there was never a formal order'.†

Health Secretary Matt Hancock also tried to paper over a lack of action on care homes when he claimed: 'Right from the start we've tried to throw a protective ring around our care homes.'‡ In fact, the opposite was true. By far the most negligent decision of the government was to allow people discharged from hospital back into care homes without being tested. Johnson again lied in the Commons when he said on 13 May: 'I can tell the House that the number of discharges from hospitals into care homes actually went down in March and April, and we had a system of testing people going into care homes.'§ The claim was again repeated by Culture Secretary Oliver Dowden on 20 May, who said testing

---

* Ibid.

† Ibid.

‡ Matt Hancock, press briefing; see Sky News (@SkyNews), '"Right from the start we've tried to throw a protective ring around our care homes"', Twitter, 15 May 2020, https://twitter.com/SkyNews/status/1261329991708684294.

§ Hansard, HC Deb, 13 May 2020, vol. 676, col. 240.

had been available to care homes 'right from the very beginning'.*

In reality, testing was only formally introduced on 15 April, as announced by Matt Hancock at the daily briefing.† This meant that for weeks thousands of potential carriers were reintroduced to care homes.

Johnson later sought to blame the care homes themselves for mistakes made by his government. On a visit to Yorkshire in early July, he said that 'too many care homes didn't really follow the procedures as they could have'.‡ This suggestion that care homes were themselves to blame produced a scathing response from Mark Adams, the chief executive of one of Britain's largest health and social care charities, Community Integrated Care: 'What we're getting is history rewritten in front of us, when you could list pages and pages of government failure, which the system has had to cope with. And to get a throwaway comment almost glibly blaming the social care system and

---

* Oliver Dowden, press briefing; see 'How much testing was done in care homes?', BBC News, 20 May 2020, https://www.bbc.co.uk/news/live/world-52733676/page/2.

† 'Health and Social Care Secretary's statement on coronavirus (COVID-19): 15 April 2020', Gov.uk, https://www.gov.uk/government/speeches/health-and-social-care-secretarys-statement-on-coronavirus-covid-19-15-april-2020.

‡ Laura Donnelly, 'Boris Johnson: Care homes didn't follow procedures correctly during coronavirus outbreak', *The Telegraph*, 6 July 2020, https://www.telegraph.co.uk/news/2020/07/06/boris-johnson-care-homes-didnt-follow-procedures-correctly-coronavirus/.

not holding your hands up for starting too late, doing the wrong things, making mistake after mistake, is just frankly unacceptable.'*

The House of Commons Public Accounts Committee's report into government policy on care homes could hardly have been more damning. It called the decision to discharge 25,000 patients from hospital into social care without first testing them a 'reckless' and 'appalling error'.† The government had taken no responsibility and to this day it continues to try to blame others on the basis of false and misleading statements.

In this chapter I have shown how this technique of blame shifting and deceit was a core part of Boris Johnson's response to coronavirus. In the next chapter I will show how this strategy stretched across almost every part of government, evolving into a determined attack on the nature of the British state itself.

---

* Ashley Cowburn, '"Travesty of leadership": Charity boss hits out at "cowardly" Boris Johnson after PM blames care homes for coronavirus deaths', *The Independent*, 7 July 2020, https://www.independent.co.uk/news/uk/politics/boris-johnson-coronavirus-care-home-deaths-a9604951.html.

† House of Commons Public Accounts Committee, *Readying the NHS and Social Care for the COVID-19 Peak*, Fourteenth Report, Session 2019–21, HC 405, 29 July 2020, p. 6, https://publications.parliament.uk/pa/cm5801/cmselect/cmpubacc/405/405.pdf.

Chapter Six

How to Destroy a Country

'I think he honestly believes that it is churlish of us
not to regard him as an exception, one who should
be free of the network of obligation which binds
everyone else.'

MARTIN HAMMOND, BORIS JOHNSON'S HOUSEMASTER
AT ETON, IN HIS SCHOOL REPORT

So far I have presented Boris Johnson as an ambitious politician whose campaigning exuberance has been replaced by
incompetence and dishonesty in high office. This picture
leaves out an essential element of the story. While there is
no doubt that Johnson is both deceitful and amoral, the
prime minister's war on the truth is part of a wider attack
on the pillars of British democracy: Parliament, the rule of
law and the civil service.

There is a reason for this. Truth and liberal democracy
are intertwined. To make rulers accountable to the people

the latter need access to objective truth. When truth is defined by the rulers themselves, the people lose all ability to pass judgement on them. The philosopher Immanuel Kant argued that lying corrupts our basic humanity because it deprives us of the ability to make rational choices.* In the political sphere, we cannot replace a poorly performing government with a potentially better one, if, by successful lying, that government has denied us the means of conceiving of one.

George Orwell made this point the central theme of his dystopian novel *1984*. The hero, Winston Smith, works for the gigantic central Ministry of Truth, whose sole purpose is to ensure that every single 'fact' available to the population supports the narrative of a wise and successful ruling party. When the enemy in the perpetual war changes from Eurasia to East Asia, every single reference to war against Eurasia is obliterated, to make East Asia the enemy all along. When the chocolate ration is reduced by the Ministry of Plenty the new amount is presented as an increase and all reference to the old (higher) amount is replaced by something lower. In the novel, the endless reframing of the 'truth' succeeds in its purpose. Citizens believe the Party propaganda even when it is contradicted in their real lives.† 'From a totalitarian point of view history is something to

---

* See Peter Oborne, *The Rise of Political Lying* (London: Free Press, 2005), p. 223.

† George Orwell, *1984* (London: Secker & Warburg, 1949), part 1, ch. 5.

be created rather than learned,' wrote Orwell, adding that totalitarianism demands 'the continuous alteration of the past, and in the long run probably demands a disbelief in the very existence of objective truth'.*

The Johnson government is not totalitarian but it already displays troubling elements of Orwell's nightmare epistemological universe. It has been caught out rewriting the past in very much the same way as Orwell's Ministry of Truth. Health Secretary Matt Hancock claimed that 16 March was 'precisely when the lockdown was started', but it was not until 23 March that Johnson told the country that people 'must' stay at home and certain businesses must close.† Another example of this was Dominic Cummings's claim that 'for years, I have warned of the dangers of pandemics'. He added: 'Last year I wrote about the possible threat of coronaviruses and the urgent need for planning.' It later emerged that this was not true and that he had secretly updated his blog in order to give authenticity to his false claim.‡

---

* George Orwell, 'The Prevention of Literature' (1946).

† Hancock did tell the House of Commons on 16 March that 'unnecessary social contact' should be avoided; see 'When did lockdown begin in the UK?', Full Fact, 22 July 2020, https://fullfact. org/health/coronavirus-lockdown-hancock-claim/.

‡ Bill Gardner and James Cook, 'Dominic Cummings's coronavirus "prediction" claim undermined after it emerges he secretly edited blog post', *The Telegraph*, 26 May 2020, https://www.telegraph.co.uk/ news/2020/05/26/dominic-cummingss-coronavirus-prediction-claim-undermined-emerges/.

Perjury is punished so heavily as an offence because justice cannot be done if witnesses tell lies, nor, conversely, if prosecutors withhold the truth. Men and women get convicted for crimes they have not committed, or escape justice when guilty. Trust in justice collapses. The same applies to politics, where habitual lying destroys faith in public life. This is the reason why lying to Parliament is (in healthy times) a career-ending offence. Parliament is there to question the decisions of ministers and hold government accountable. It can't do its job if ministers lie, supply false information and withhold the truth.

Truthlessness matters for the same reason in the civil service. Officials are employed to give fair and scrupulous advice to ministers. Without that advice, governments become easy prey for cronyism and special interests.

Finally, truth matters for democracy itself. Political deceit is theft. Lying politicians do not (necessarily) steal our money or our possessions. But they always steal our rights as citizens by causing us to vote on the basis of misleading information. This in turn strips us of the ability to reach informed political choices. Governments who lie to voters are treating us as dupes rather than equals. Our rulers expect us to comply with their laws and decrees, to pay the taxes they devise, to make the sacrifices they exhort on us, even sometimes to die in war. In a democratic society, such obedience has to be earned. When ministers use lies and misrepresentation they fray the bonds of loyalty we owe to the state, opening the way to anarchy.

These are all simple points which have been taught to generations of schoolchildren. They embody ancient and (until very recently) generally accepted wisdom. Something has gone wrong when those who lead us need reminding of these basic points.

Johnson does not value integrity. He acts as if he does not even know what it is. This means that he has embarked on an experiment in government with huge consequences for democracy. The most illustrious victim (so far) is the Cabinet secretary, the most senior civil servant in Britain and the ultimate symbol of public integrity.

DISPOSING OF THE CABINET SECRETARY

I described at the end of the chapter above how government briefers arranged a vicious and dishonest whispering campaign at the height of the coronavirus pandemic, using media allies to place the responsibility for government failures on others, while leaving ministers with clean hands.

This was not simply despicable. It marked a serious breach of the doctrine of ministerial responsibility through which Britain had been governed in the twentieth century. Ministers were the public face of their departments, which meant they took responsibility for the successes.

The classic example was the resignation of Lord Carrington as foreign secretary after the invasion of the Falkland Islands in 1982. There is no evidence that

Carrington was personally at fault for the debacle, and almost nobody held him responsible. But Carrington (who had been decorated for bravery during the Second World War) could not be dissuaded.* Around the same time, the prime minister, Margaret Thatcher, had great difficulty persuading her home secretary, Willie Whitelaw (who had also seen distinguished war service), not to resign after an intruder broke into the Queen's bedroom at Buckingham Palace.

A more recent case concerns Estelle Morris, who resigned as education secretary in October 2002. Morris had promised to step down if targets for exam results were not met.† When they were not, she resigned, even though Prime Minister Tony Blair had put her under no pressure. In her resignation letter she wrote: 'I have learned what I am good at and also what I am less good at. I am good at dealing with the issues and in communicating to the teaching profession. I am less good at strategic management of a huge department and I am not good at dealing with the modern media.'‡

---

* The apogee of standards in twentieth-century public life was reached in the so-called Crichel Down affair of 1954 when the agriculture minister, Sir Thomas Dugdale, was forced to resign over maladministration by his department for which he had no responsibility. Significantly, Carrington, his junior minister at the time, also offered to resign, but this was not required.

† 'Estelle Morris resigns', *The Telegraph*, 23 October 2002, https://www.telegraph.co.uk/news/1411041/Estelle-Morris-resigns.html.

‡ Ibid.

There was a basic decency at work here. Ministers took credit they did not always deserve for work by civil servants, so they should take the blame as well. Morris didn't feel that she was competent at her job and her sense of public duty compelled her to say so. Her resignation was just as honourable (though not remembered so widely) as Carrington's. Her conduct bears comparison with Boris Johnson's education secretary, Gavin Williamson, who resisted pressure to go in the summer of 2020 when exam results were arbitrarily marked down in a fiasco that threatened to deprive thousands of young people of a university place. Williamson tried to lay off the responsibility on the exam regulator, Ofqual,* while reports emerged in the press that the permanent secretary at the Department for Education was being lined up to take the blame.

More pertinently, public servants were contractually banned from speaking in public and therefore unable to defend themselves from attack. This made smear campaigns of the kind the Johnson machine launched against the Cabinet secretary, Sir Mark Sedwill, and others especially cowardly.

From the moment that Boris Johnson became prime minister, Sedwill was doomed. There was nothing personal about this. The problem was the post he occupied.

---

* Camilla Turner, Catherine Neilan and Charles Hymas, 'Gavin Williamson blames Ofqual as he confirms A-level and GCSE exam results U-turn', *The Telegraph*, 17 August 2020, https://www.telegraph. co.uk/news/2020/08/17/gavin-williamson-blames-ofqual-confirms-a-level-gcse-exam-results/.

The Cabinet secretary is – or at any rate was, until the arrival of the Johnson government – a momentous figure in British public life. The post embodies the qualities of discretion, intellectual scruple, honesty and impartiality which lie at the heart of the idea of British statecraft. Johnson and the coterie of advisers he brought with him into Downing Street either despised these qualities or simply did not understand them.

There have been only thirteen Cabinet secretaries since the post was invented in 1916. That in itself signals their importance within the British state. During that period they have been the voice of integrity and guardian of the distinction between party and state. Those who were thought too close to their prime ministers of the day were criticised, as with Sir William Armstrong and Ted Heath. The Cabinet secretary is at the heart of the British system of government. This does not rely, as the US system does, on formal checks and balances to guarantee integrity and root out wrongdoing. It depends on informal conventions, especially a system of sharply defined dividing lines between ministers and officials.

On the one hand you have the official: anonymous, self-effacing and permanent. The official makes one important act of renunciation.* He or she is banned from taking part in

---

* Patrick Diamond, 'Ministers, civil servants, and the erosion of the "public service bargain" in Whitehall', LSE, 9 March 2020, https://blogs.lse.ac.uk/politicsandpolicy/public-service-bargain/. According to Bernard Schaffer, author of *The Administrative Factor* (1973) – a

political activity and formally owes allegiance to the Crown. She or he is, however, licensed to speak 'truth to power', that is, to tell ministers awkward information they might not like to hear. In the elegant words of the late *Guardian* columnist Hugo Young, the civil service believes 'that it represents and personifies the seamless integrity of past, present and future government rolled indistinguishably into one'.

The task of an official is, nevertheless, to carry out the lawful orders of elected politicians. Ultimately, they will do so, although they have the power (increasingly exercised in modern times) to insist on a written order making clear the responsibility of ministers. This is why impartiality matters. It is a matter of professional pride that civil servants should work for governments of whatever party with equal competence and enthusiasm. This is important in Britain because (unlike in the United States) the machinery of state is supposed to be neutral.

For a civil servant such as Sedwill, facts should carry no partisan or party–political colour. They can be independently established, verified and assessed. For the Johnson government by contrast, truth has become a weapon. This means that Johnson and his colleagues are redefining the idea of truth as it has enabled public discourse in Britain for the last 200 years.

---

book attempting to tackle the problems arising from modernisation – officials 'exchanged overt partisanship, some political rights and a public political profile in return for permanent careers, honours, and a six-hour working day'.

THE DESTRUCTION OF THE PUBLIC DOMAIN

Sedwill's departure was handled carefully. Johnson did not sack the Cabinet secretary. That is impossible under civil service rules, explicitly designed to prohibit political interference in civil service appointments. But the Cabinet secretary was pushed out after a media briefing campaign. This was nevertheless an event of immense constitutional importance because it sent the message through Whitehall that the machinery of state, and its most important official, were losing their non-partisan status and shifting into political hands.

Curiously enough, although the far left of the Labour Party has regularly fulminated against the alleged bias of top civil servants and threatened to replace them with ideological sympathisers, it is the right wing of the Tory Party which has done far more to achieve this. It is a key part of what has been a cherished ambition of theirs for many years: the destruction of what the political philosopher David Marquand christened the 'public domain'. He described this eloquently:

> The private domain has always been with us; and Adam Smith was probably right in thinking that the 'truck, barter and exchange' of the market domain are natural to human beings. But there is nothing natural about the public domain. It is a gift of history, and of fairly recent history at that. It is literally a priceless gift. The goods of

the public domain cannot be valued by market criteria, but they are no less precious for that. They include fair trials, welcoming public spaces, free public libraries, subsidised opera, mutual building societies, safe food, the broadcasts of the BBC World Service, the lobbying of Amnesty International, clean water, impartial public administration, disinterested scholarship, blood donors, magistrates, the minimum wage, the Pennine Way and the rulings of the Health and Safety Executive. Less obviously, they also include liberty – not in the familiar sense of freedom to pursue private interests, but in the classical republican sense of freedom from domination. In the public domain, market power is over-ridden; citizens bow the knee to nobody.*

At the heart of the public domain is truth. This is because it needs strong institutions including Parliament, the rule of law and an impartial state machinery which citizens can trust. After the departure of Sedwill there was no longer any doubt that the Johnson government was set on the destruction of these institutions.

An early victim was Sir Philip Rutnam at the Home Office, after clashes with the home secretary, Priti Patel.† In

---

* David Marquand, *Decline of the Public* (Cambridge: Polity, 2004), pp. 32–3.

† Rajeev Syal, 'Priti Patel bullying row: ex-Home Office chief launches tribunal claim', *The Guardian*, 20 April 2020, https://www.theguardian.com/politics/2020/apr/20/priti-patel-bullying-

his resignation statement he said that he had been the 'target of a vicious and orchestrated campaign against him'.* There was no reason to disbelieve him. *The Times* quoted 'allies' of the home secretary saying: 'If this were any other environment Philip Rutnam would not only be sacked, he'd be denied a pension. The lack of accountability in the civil service is deeply troubling and the prime minister will not accept this in the long term.'

The Sun ('Britain must be governed by elected ministers – not bleating bureaucrats like Sir Philip Rutnam') and the *Telegraph* ('spends his time politicking rather than running the actual department') were just as brutal.† With

---

row-ex-home-office-chief-philip-rutnam-launches-tribunal-claim. Rutnam resigned from his role as permanent secretary to the Home Office on 29 February 2020. He had previously filed a report with the Cabinet Office concerning Patel's alleged bullying behaviour, saying she belittled officials in meetings and made unreasonable demands on staff. On 20 April, Rutnam lodged an employment tribunal claim, saying that he was forced from his job for exposing her behaviour. Priti Patel emphatically denied these charges of bullying. Reports in November 2020 revealed the enquiry into the bullying allegations found evidence of 'behaviour that can be described as bullying', in breach of the ministerial code. Oliver Wright, '"Bullying" report chief Alex Allan quits after PM backs Priti Patel', *The Times*, 20 November 2020, https://www.thetimes.co.uk/article/bullying-report-chief-alex-allan-quits-after-pm-backs-priti-patel-5jgtf7fqg.

* Aaron Walawalkar, 'Home Office chief Sir Philip Rutnam quits over Priti Patel "bullying"', *The Guardian*, 29 February 2020, https://www.theguardian.com/politics/2020/feb/29/home-office-chief-sir-philip-rutnam-quits-over-priti-patel-bullying.

† Dave Wooding, 'PRITI VICIOUS: Priti Patel's top civil servant QUITS with astonishing attack on home secretary over "vicious campaign against him"', *The Sun*, 29 February 2020, https://

Rutnam gone, attention turned to Sir Simon McDonald, permanent secretary at the Foreign Office, who announced his departure, reportedly 'at the request' of Boris Johnson, in June.‡ By September 2020, no less than six permanent secretaries – Whitehall's most senior civil servants – were either gone or on their way out.† According to the *Daily Telegraph*, a frequent receptacle for pro-government bile, Tom Scholar at the Treasury was on a '"s—list" of permanent secretaries No. 10 wants replaced over claims that they are significantly at odds with Tory ministers and advisers.'‡ At the time this book went to print, Tom Scholar remained in place. Previous prime ministers had taken against senior civil servants, but never in such speed or on such a scale, nor accompanied by such merciless briefing.§

---

www.thesun.co.uk/news/11068701/home-office-philip-rutnam-resigns/; Charles Hymas, 'MI5 dragged into Home Office civil war as officials deny "false" claims against Priti Patel', *The Telegraph*, 23 February 2020, https://www.telegraph.co.uk/politics/2020/02/23/mi5-dragged-home-office-civil-war-officials-deny-false-claims/.

‡ 'Boris Johnson asks Foreign Office chief to stand down', *BBC News*, 19 June 2020, https://www.bbc.co.uk/news/uk/politics-53111095.

† These were: Sedwill, Rutnam, Sir Jonathan Jones of the Government Legal Department, Jonathan Slater of the Department for Education, Sir Simon McDonald of the Foreign Office, Sir Richard Heaton of the Ministry of Justice, and Melanie Dawes of the Ministry of Housing, Communities & Local Government.

‡ Edward Malnick, 'Top civil servants on Tories' "hit list"'. *The Telegraph*, 22 February 2020, https://www.telegraph.co.uk/politics/2020/02/22/top-civil-servants-tories-hit-list/.

§ Margaret Thatcher was accused of engineering the removal of Sir Douglas Wass, permanent secretary at the Treasury. It took her two years. Tony

By midsummer 2020, it was obvious that Boris Johnson and his clique were determined to dismantle the system of administrative integrity famously instigated by Stafford Northcote (later to be chancellor of the Exchequer) and C. E. Trevelyan (then permanent secretary to the Treasury) in the mid-nineteenth century. More than any other single event, these two Victorian grandees created the modern British state. They eradicated ancient ties of connection, nepotism and family, while establishing dividing lines between public and private, and party and state. The new system was constructed to prevent politicians from enriching themselves and rewarding relations, clients and dependants. They were part of a close-knit congregation of public figures of high moral stature which included W. E. Gladstone (then chancellor and later four times prime minister) and Benjamin Jowett, theologian and later master of Balliol College, Oxford, who set the tone for public administration which lasted until the start of the twenty-first century.* They created a system where ministers not only had to avoid misbehaviour but to avoid even the faintest suggestion of it.

These great men would have regarded Prime Minister Johnson and his squalid associates with horror. It is not simply the habitual deceit, the lying to Parliament, the

---

Blair tolerated briefing against his Cabinet secretary Sir Richard Wilson, who nevertheless left in his own time and of his own accord.

* Peter Hennessy, *Whitehall* (London: Pimlico, 2001).

bullying of vulnerable subordinates.* Downing Street cronyism also represents a two-fingered repudiation of the principles underlying the Northcote–Trevelyan system.

Repeatedly the Johnson administration has been embarrassed by allegations that government contracts have gone to business people with close connections to ministers and advisers or lacking any relevant expertise. In January 2020 Housing Secretary Robert Jenrick unexpectedly overturned official advice and granted planning permission for a £1 billion development in Tower Hamlets, east London.

---

* On 29 August 2019, Sonia Khan, a Treasury media adviser, was accused of lying about her interactions with staff close to the former chancellor Philip Hammond, after Dominic Cummings reportedly found evidence on her personal mobile phone. She was escorted from Downing Street by armed police after being sacked by Cummings. Later, in a meeting with special advisers, an article in *The Guardian* reported Cummings saying: 'If you don't like how I run things, there's the door.' Chancellor Sajid Javid, who was not aware of the sacking of his adviser until afterwards, accused Johnson of cultivating a 'culture of fear'. In February 2020, Khan launched legal proceedings for unfair dismissal.

Javid himself did not last long under Johnson's premiership. He resigned on 13 February 2020, after Johnson said he would have to replace all of his advisers if he was to stay in the role. See Rowena Mason, Heather Stewart and Peter Walker, 'Sajid Javid resigns as chancellor in Boris Johnson reshuffle', *The Guardian*, 13 February 2020, https://www.theguardian.com/politics/2020/feb/13/sajid-javid-resigns-as-chancellor-amid-boris-johnson-reshuffle; Kate Proctor, 'Adviser sacked by Cummings may have case for unfair dismissal – expert', *The Guardian*, 1 September 2019, https://www.theguardian.com/politics/2019/sep/01/adviser-sacked-by-cummings-may-have-case-for-unfair-dismissal-expert; Kate Proctor, '"Culture of fear" claims as Javid confronts PM over adviser's sacking', *The Guardian*, 30 August 2019, https://www.theguardian.com/politics/2019/aug/30/sajid-javid-confronts-boris-johnson-over-advisers-sacking.

The move saved the developer, the one-time newspaper owner and pornographer Richard Desmond, £45 million in local taxes – and Tower Hamlets is one of the poorest parts of Britain. Or it would have done, had the minister's decision not been overturned on appeal. High Court documents show that what Jenrick did was 'unlawful by reason of apparent bias'.*

Only a few weeks earlier, Jenrick had sat next to Desmond at a Conservative fundraising event. A few weeks after the planning approval was given, Desmond made a modest £12,000 donation to Conservative funds. When the scandal broke, Jenrick said he'd refused to discuss the planning application with Desmond at the dinner.† Then he admitted he had watched a promotion for the development on Desmond's mobile phone.‡

The wretched Jenrick was open to exactly the charges of conflict of interest and cronyism which Stafford Northcote and Charles Trevelyan had moved mountains to guard against. Boris Johnson's government was hurtling Britain

---

* Jon Sharman, 'Robert Jenrick showed "apparent bias" in approving Conservative Party donor's housing development', *The Independent*, 27 May 2020, https://www.independent.co.uk/news/uk/politics/robert-jenrick-bias-tower-hamlets-westferry-printworks-richard-desmond-northern-shell-a9534941.html.

† 'Westferry planning row: Jenrick texted property developer, documents show', BBC News, 25 June 2020, https://www.bbc.co.uk/news/uk-politics-53172995.

‡ Heather Stewart and Rajeev Syal, 'The Robert Jenrick planning row explained', *The Guardian*, 24 June 2020, https://www.theguardian.com/politics/2020/jun/24/robert-jenrick-planning-row-the-key-questions-answered.

back towards the pre-modern system where public men had no room for selfless public service and interpreted office as a means of rewarding relations, clients and dependants, while in due course enriching themselves.

WARNING SIGNS

Johnson and the team that surrounds him do not believe that ordinary standards apply to them. Martin Hammond, Johnson's housemaster when he was at Eton, wrote in a letter to Johnson's father: 'I think he honestly believes that it is churlish of us not to regard him as an exception, one who should be free of the network of obligation which binds everyone else.'*

The warning signs were all there *before* Johnson became prime minister. Take Johnson's conduct after resigning as foreign secretary in July 2018. First of all he refused to leave his official Carlton House residence for three weeks, despite warnings from the permanent secretary.† Within

---

* Zamira Rahim, 'Boris Johnson showed "disgracefully cavalier" attitude to studies, school letter reveals', *The Independent*, 4 October 2019, https://www.independent.co.uk/news/uk/politics/boris-johnson-rory-stewart-eton-college-letters-live-a9142711.html.

† The *Daily Mail* reported that Sir Simon McDonald, permanent secretary at the Foreign and Commonwealth Office, dispatched text messages to Johnson telling him to leave. The first, sent on 9 July, told Johnson that the Cabinet Office would like him out within 48 hours. Four days later, with Johnson still on the premises, McDonald sent another message saying, 'Time is passing and I have still not seen a plan. So I'd be grateful for an update, please.' He reminded Johnson

a week of resigning, he had struck a contract to write a weekly column with the *Daily Telegraph* without taking the basic precaution of seeking advice from the Advisory Committee on Business Appointments (ACOBA).* The committee chair, Baroness Browning, wrote to Johnson on 8 August: 'The committee considers it unacceptable that you signed a contract with the *Telegraph* and your appointment was announced before you had sought and obtained advice from the committee, as was incumbent upon you on leaving office under the Government's Business Appointment Rules.'† The letter went on to note that the rules were contained within the Ministerial Code and he

---

that he had yet to surrender his diplomatic passport, government-issue laptop, iPads and phone. Six days later, the permanent secretary wrote again to complain that he had still not been given a departure date. See 'Fourth senior civil servant announces exit in six months', BBC News, 9 July 2020, https://www.bbc.co.uk/news/uk-politics-53351672; Jason Groves, 'Boris Johnson "ignored" official letters telling him to leave his £20million taxpayer-funded Government apartment for three weeks after he resigned as Foreign Secretary', *MailOnline*, 13 December 2018, https://www.dailymail.co.uk/news/article-6494031/Boris-Johnson-ignored-official-letters-telling-leave-20million-Government-apartment.html.

* Leighton Andrews, 'Brexit, Cabinet Norms and the Ministerial Code: Are We Living in a post-Nolan Era?' *Political Quarterly* 91:1 (2020), pp. 125–33, at p. 126. As far as I can tell this telling episode was covered by neither *The Times* nor the *Telegraph*.

† Freedom of Information Act 2000 decision notice, FS50795901, 15 October 2019, p. 4, https://ico.org.uk/media/action-weve-taken/decision-notices/2019/2616091/fs50795901.pdf; Andrews, 'Brexit, Cabinet Norms and the Ministerial Code', p. 126.

was guilty of 'a failure to comply with your duty'.* This was especially powerful from ACOBA, which has been regularly denounced as a feeble watchdog and too tolerant of the passage of ministers and senior public servants into lucrative private sector positions where they can profit from official knowledge.†

In December 2018 the House of Commons Standards Committee blasted Johnson for his 'over-casual' failure to declare £52,000 in expenses.‡ The parliamentary commissioner for standards said it was 'a lack of attention to House requirements, rather than inadvertent error'.§ The Tory MPs who elected Boris Johnson Tory leader a few months later were thus well aware that he was contemptuous of the basic principles that are supposed to govern public life. The same applies to the newspapers which endorsed his leadership bid – *The Sun*, the *Telegraph*, *The Times*, the *Daily Mail*, the *Express* and the *Evening Standard*. By supporting him they were making a public statement that they did not care either.¶

---

* Andrews, 'Brexit, Cabinet Norms and the Ministerial Code', p. 126; Freedom of Information Act 2000 decision notice, FS50795901, 15 October 2019, p. 8.

† See especially the 'Revolving Doors' section in *Private Eye*.

‡ Andrews, 'Brexit, Cabinet Norms and the Ministerial Code', p. 127.

§ Ibid., p. 127.

¶ *The Times*, the *Telegraph* and *The Sun* all notably backed Johnson during his leadership bid in July 2019. Although *The Times*, in its endorsement, acknowledged his 'lack of attention to detail' and the fact that questions have been raised about his 'honesty,

Principles of Public Life

In fairness, Boris Johnson is not the first prime minister to break rules.* Human nature being what it is, many of his predecessors in Downing Street have tried to get around them. But the spirit of Northcote–Trevelyan has, until now, been strong enough to survive.

In the early 1990s, John Major's embattled Conservative government was hit hard by a series of scandals calling into question the integrity of the government, of which the

---

loyalty and personal relationships', none of these publications made direct reference to these examples of Johnson acting in contempt of the Nolan principles. See 'The Times view on the next prime minister: Boris Johnson at No 10', *The Times*, 6 July 2019, https://www.thetimes.co.uk/article/the-times-view-on-the-next-prime-minister-boris-johnson-at-no-10-njpzrff8v; 'Boris Johnson is Mr Brexit. Elect him PM and give him a chance to deliver it', *The Telegraph*, 4 July 2019, https://www.telegraph.co.uk/opinion/2019/07/04/boris-johnson-mr-brexit-elect-pm-give-chance-deliver/; Priti Patel, 'I'll back Boris Johnson to be our PM and make Britain greater by delivering Brexit', *The Sun*, 9 June 2019, https://www.thesun.co.uk/news/9251918/boris-johnson-tory-leadership-race-priti-patel-opinion/.

* See Frances Donaldson, *The Marconi Scandal* (London: Bloomsbury, [1962] 2011). One of Britain's greatest politicians, David Lloyd George, was nearly destroyed by accusations of insider trading in the Marconi scandal of 1912. Later as prime minister he blatantly sold honours for political donations (which was then regarded as outrageous, although the Tories in his coalition government took half the receipts). Lloyd George was forgiven much for his achievements, including national insurance, old age pensions, financial reform and winning the Great War. Boris Johnson cannot match this record in office to date, nor is he ever likely to. This may make it all the more important to him to collapse the standards by which British prime ministers are judged.

most serious was the so-called arms-to-Iraq affair. (This was unfair on John Major personally, since this was an inheritance from the Thatcher government of the 1980s.) For many weeks, this long-forgotten episode dominated politics. The directors of a Midlands engineering firm, Matrix Churchill, were charged with illegally exporting military materials while pretending they were for civilian purposes. The trial collapsed after trade minister Alan Clark admitted in court that he had known all along that the Iraqi order would be used to make munitions. A famous exchange took place when Clark was asked about an official note which recorded him saying that the orders would be used for general manufacturing purposes. Clark replied:

> Well, it's our old friend being economical, isn't it?
> Q. With the truth?
> A. With the actualité.*

In the fallout from Clark's remarks, it emerged that in its eagerness to sell arms to Saddam Hussein, the Thatcher government had breached official guidelines, then concealed this from Parliament. Meanwhile, it separately emerged that Tory MPs – including Neil Hamilton, another former trade minister – had been paid to ask Commons questions. Major (a moral giant compared to the current prime minister) adopted the only possible course

---

* Marquand, *Decline of the Public*, p. 7.

of action. He commissioned a law lord, Michael Nolan, to launch an investigation. The resulting report was a model of clarity.* Besides insisting that MPs should not be allowed to act as paid agents for lobbyists and introducing an anti-sleaze parliamentary commissioner, Lord Nolan unveiled seven principles which, so he said, should govern public life.

They are a magnificent statement of how a country (or any organisation) should be governed, providing the ethical grounding for matters including misleading Parliament, MPs' outside interests, business appointments for former ministers, ministerial accountability, impartiality of the civil service and neutrality of the monarch. Nolan demanded selflessness, integrity, objectivity, accountability, openness, honesty and leadership: 'Holders of public office should promote and support these principles by leadership and example.'† In essence he reaffirmed Northcote–Trevelyan. He was given a committee to promote them. It is still named after him, but has become a pale, powerless spectre.

The Nolan principles are almost scriptural in their simplicity. It's heart-breaking to read them today. Not one of them is being observed, and there is no serious attempt

---

* *Standards in Public Life: First Report of the Committee on Standards in Public Life, vol. 1: Report*, Cm 2850-I, May 1995, https://assets. publishing.service.gov.uk/government/uploads/system/uploads/ attachment_data/file/336919/1stInquiryReport.pdf.

† https://assets.publishing.service.gov.uk/government/uploads/system/ uploads/attachment_data/file/361338/seven-principles-of-public-life.pdf.

to enforce them. Breaking them carries no consequences. There's one standard for ministers and another for those in the outside world. Ministers can lie to Parliament but escape rebuke. They can bully and harass staff and get away with it. They can undermine civil servants and not pay the price. They can award contracts to cronies and nobody minds. The Nolan principles today look quaint, irrelevant and out of date. There is a moral emergency in British public life.

Chapter Seven

THE FAILURE OF THE BRITISH PRESS

'A free press is the unsleeping guardian of every other right that free men prize; it is the most dangerous foe of tyranny ... where free institutions are indigenous to the soil and men have the habit of liberty, the press will continue to be the Fourth Estate, the vigilant guardian of the rights of the ordinary citizen.'

SIR WINSTON CHURCHILL

British newspapers have played a critical role in the production, authentication, dissemination and, most important of all, the normalisation of the lies, fabrications and smears issued by the Johnson political machine. In this chapter I will show how they became part of the official apparatus of deceit.

Johnson's government was a media class government. The prime minister had been one of the most brilliant journalists of his time, destined to become a famous editor, a job which would have fitted him like a glove, had he not entered politics. The same was true of his senior colleague (and rival) Michael Gove. Instigating, organising and manipulating these two front men was Dominic Cummings, formidable political public relations campaigner and the prime minister's 'senior adviser'.*

Between them they brought into government the strengths and weaknesses of the media world they came from. On the one hand, brilliance, verve, style, wit and an intuitive understanding of the darker side of human nature. On the other hand, a readiness to distort, misrepresent, smear and fabricate.

Future generations are bound to ask why Johnson's record as a liar, charlatan and cheat did not prove fatal on his way into Downing Street. It would have done for earlier generations. The answer is complex, and I will return to the question in the final chapter, but one reason is that the mainstream press ignored Johnson's lies. Newspapers might highlight the occasional inaccuracy, but this tended to be done in the deferential manner of a bank manager drawing attention to a bounced cheque from a cherished customer. Fleet Street decided that Johnson's lying was of little interest to readers.

---

* His official title was chief adviser to the prime minister of the United Kingdom, a position he has held between July 2019 and late 2020.

The truth was that press barons were determined to install the troika of Johnson, Gove and Cummings in Downing Street.* Michael Gove was the special protégé of the American tycoon Rupert Murdoch, owner of *The Sun*, *The Times* and Fox News, the most formidable media backer of Donald Trump. When Murdoch's News International group was on its knees following revelations of criminal phone hacking, Gove came eloquently to the defence of press freedom at the Leveson inquiry. Murdoch did not forget: Gove and his wife Sarah Vine were invited to his wedding to the former model Jerry Hall.

Murdoch also supported Johnson, but his principal sponsors were the Barclay brothers, shadowy owners of the *Daily Telegraph*, house journal for the Conservative Party.† 'Many congratulations to Boris Johnson who has of course just been appointed Prime Minister,' enthused the paper when he entered 10 Downing Street. 'Boris is the first *Telegraph* journalist since Sir Winston Churchill to lead the country.'

Associated Newspapers, owners of the *Mail on Sunday* and the *Daily Mail*, which employed Sarah Vine, also backed Johnson. Together these three groups accounted for more

---

* Michael Gove was appointed chancellor of the Duchy of Lancaster on 24 July 2019. Though this book has concentrated on the integrity of the prime minister, Gove was another habitual liar.

† The *Daily Telegraph* paid Johnson £22,916.66 a month for a column in the paper. See 'Register of Members' Financial Interests as at 10 February 2020', https://publications.parliament.uk/pa/cm/cmregmem/200210/200210.pdf.

than 30 per cent of British newspaper readers.* All their titles backed Johnson. The same applied to the *Evening Standard*, which serves London, an area of predominantly Labour and Remain voters. Under the ownership of Evgeny Lebedev it became an unlikely ally of the Tories, backing Johnson for both Conservative leader and prime minister.

Yet editors knew perfectly well what the prime minister was like – after all *The Times* had actually sacked him for fabricating the quotation about Piers Gaveston (see page 54). But they backed him regardless. The *Telegraph* supported Johnson even though, like *The Times*, it had direct experience of his chronic carelessness with facts. In an article for the *Daily Telegraph* in January 2019 Johnson claimed that 'the so-called no-deal option' for Brexit 'is by some margin preferred by the British public'. This was false. Unfortunately for Johnson a reader complained to the Independent Press Standards Organisation. According to the regulator, the *Telegraph* stood by Johnson on the grounds that his article was 'clearly comically polemical'

---

* The *Daily Mail* makes up 25.9 per cent of the Monday to Saturday readership. The *Mail on Sunday* makes up 23.1 per cent of the Sunday readership. The Telegraph Media Group has a 6 per cent share of newspaper readership. See 'Figures reveal the Daily Mail and the Mail on Sunday continue to outperform the national newspaper market', DMG Media, 22 October 2019, https://www.dmgmedia.co.uk/news/figures-reveal-the-daily-mail-and-the-mail-on-sunday-continue-to-outperform-the-national-newspaper-market/; Freddy Mayhew, 'The biggest newspaper groups in the UK: Rothermere and Murdoch control two thirds of market', *Press Gazette*, 18 August 2020, https://www.pressgazette.co.uk/biggest-news-groups-uk/.

and would not be read as a 'serious, empirical, in-depth analysis of hard factual matters'.[*]

The open support offered by British newspapers for Johnson was of course welcome. Far more important was their collective decision to turn a blind eye to stories that would damage the prime minister. For example, the mainstream press paid almost no attention to Johnson's habitual lying, in sharp contrast to their treatment of the Labour leader, Jeremy Corbyn, who was subject to constant attack. Problems with Tory Party funding, the prime minister's finances and his family life were ignored and only surfaced long after the election.[†]

---

[*] The complaint was upheld and the *Telegraph* was forced to publish a correction. IPSO noted that the *Telegraph* 'had not provided any data which supported the author's claim ... that a no-deal Brexit was the option preferred "by some margin" over the three options listed' (00154-19 *Stirling v The Daily Telegraph*, IPSO, https://www. ipso.co.uk/rulings-and-resolution-statements/ruling/?id=00154-19.

[†] Oliver Wright, Francis Elliott and Matt Chorley, 'Overburdened, underpaid and "misery on his face": Boris Johnson gets the blues', *The Times*, 19 September 2020, https://www.thetimes.co.uk/article/ overburdened-underpaid-and-misery-on-his-face-boris-johnson-gets-the-blues-r9jl63m2q; Jack Wright, 'As if Brexit and coronavirus were not enough ... Boris is "broke"! "Subdued" PM "worries about money" after salary shrank to £150k – "leaving him unable to afford housekeeper or nanny for baby Wilfred" (while supporting four of his other six children)', *MailOnline*, 19 September 2020, https://www.dailymail.co.uk/news/article-8750253/Subdued-Boris-Johnson-worries-money-salary-shrunk-150k.html. Another example came when Paul Dacre, chairman and editor in chief of Associated Newspapers, was given the *Spectator* diary the week Johnson became prime minister. He wrote: 'So the party of family values has chosen as leader a man of whom to say he has the morals of an alley cat

This marked a sharp breach from the textbook theory that the media plays an important cleansing role in holding power to account and uncovering corruption, lying and deceit. The former journalist and prime minister Sir Winston Churchill said: 'A free press is the unsleeping guardian of every other right that free men prize; it is the most dangerous foe of tyranny ... where free institutions are indigenous to the soil and men have the habit of liberty, the press will continue to be the Fourth Estate, the vigilant guardian of the rights of the ordinary citizen.'[*]

But Britain's major newspaper groups made the careful and deliberate choice not to be vigilant when it came to Johnson. This was a double standard.[†] Had Corbyn been

---

would be to libel the feline species. Thus the Tories, with two women PMs to their credit, have achieved another historic first: scuppering the belief – argued by the *Daily Mail* in my 26 years as editor – that politicians with scandalous private lives cannot hold high office. I make no comment on this, or about the 31-year-old minx who is the current Boris Johnson bedwarmer, but ask you instead to spare a thought for Petronella's abortion, Helen's love child, Marina's humiliation and her four children's agony.' The reporting of Johnson's family in *Mail* newspapers did not at any stage reflect the strong views Dacre shared with *Spectator* readers.

[*] Winston Churchill, 1949, quoted in Tim Luckhurst, 'Britain's press must remain free', *The Telegraph*, 24 October 2012, https://www. telegraph.co.uk/news/uknews/leveson-inquiry/9630793/Britains-press-must-remain-free.html.

[†] Of course there were stories written by the right-wing press which undermined Johnson. The most notable example concerned the technology entrepreneur Jennifer Arcuri. The *Sunday Times* revealed that Johnson had failed to declare a series of potential conflicts of interest over a close friendship with the American former model

sacked twice for lying, newspaper readers would never have heard the end of it. And rightly so. The past is the best guide to the future. If a man steals from his employers, he is likely to do so again. If he lies to them, he most likely will do so again. The mainstream British press bears a heavy culpability for the inexorable rise of Boris Johnson.

BRITISH JOURNALISTS COLLABORATE

It was not simply that the mainstream media were careful to play down, if not entirely ignore, Johnson's lies. Many senior journalists went a step further. They actively collaborated with Downing Street in order to distribute false information helpful to Johnson's cause. This began almost from the moment Boris Johnson entered Downing Street. By mid-August, within a few weeks of Johnson taking office, Downing Street was mounting a virulent smear

during his time as London mayor. Arcuri, with whom it later transpired Johnson had an affair ('Jennifer Arcuri "admits to Boris Johnson affair"', *The Guardian*, 17 October 2020, https://www. theguardian.com/politics/2020/oct/16/jennifer-arcuri-admits-to-boris-johnson-affair), was given a total of £126,000 in public money and privileged access to three official overseas trade missions led by Johnson. Though no criminal investigation followed the revelations, the story, which dominated the media for weeks, was deeply embarrassing for Johnson and raised further questions about his character.

However, the fact remains that Johnson was handed a relatively easy ride in the right-wing press, especially when compared to the near-daily stories attacking Jeremy Corbyn's character and casting doubt on his ability to be Britain's prime minister.

operation against Philip Hammond, who had stepped down as chancellor of the Exchequer when Johnson became leader, and was now seen as an enemy.

It is worth looking closely at this sordid episode because it shows the Johnson method in action. At the heart of the attack on Hammond was a lie, devised to discredit an opponent. This strategy also needed senior journalists to play along by putting their own reputations (and those of the newspapers and media organisations they worked for) behind Downing Street's falsehoods and smears. Meanwhile, Johnson was happy to abuse the reputation and integrity of Downing Street to give respectability to smears and fabrications.

The Hammond story began on 18 August 2019 after the *Sunday Times* leaked a Treasury dossier ('Yellowhammer') warning of the painful short-term disruption that would confront Britain in the event of a no-deal Brexit.* This story was embarrassing for Downing Street because it undermined its core strategy, threatening a no-deal Brexit. The government hit back, saying Yellowhammer was an 'old document'.†

---

* Rosamund Urwin and Caroline Wheeler, 'Operation Chaos: Whitehall's secret no-deal Brexit preparations leaked', *Sunday Times*, 18 August 2019, https://www.thetimes.co.uk/article/operation-chaos-whitehalls-secret-no-deal-brexit-plan-leaked-j6ntwvhll.

† Rowena Mason, 'No 10 furious at leak of paper predicting shortages after no-deal Brexit', *The Guardian*, 18 August 2019, https://www.theguardian.com/politics/2019/aug/18/number-10-furious-leak-document-predicting-no-deal-brexit-shortages; 'Brexit: No-deal dossier shows worst-case scenario – Gove', BBC News, 18 August 2019, https://www.bbc.co.uk/news/uk-politics-49388402.

This claim, it soon emerged, was false.* It was made first by Michael Gove,† minister in charge of Brexit preparations, and later by Tory chairman James Cleverly.‡

At this point 'a senior Number 10 source' went into action alongside Gove, briefing journalists that the Yellowhammer dossier was out of date.§ But this Downing Street 'source' added a second lie. This was the vicious twist that the dossier had been 'deliberately leaked by a former minister to influence discussions with EU leaders'.¶ Such a claim was deadly because the Downing Street source was implying that a minister in the Theresa May government

---

* 'The leaked Operation Yellowhammer document was an "old document"', Boris Johnson Lies, 18 August 2019, https:// boris-johnson-lies.com/the-leaked-operation-yellowhammer-document-was-an-old-document.

† Gove said: 'Operation Yellowhammer is the name that the government has given for planning for absolutely the worst case in the event of a no-deal Brexit. And it's also important to recognise that this is an old document. Since it was published and circulated the government have taken significant additional steps to ensure that we're prepared to leave on 31 October, deal or no deal' ('Brexit: No-deal dossier shows worst-case scenario – Gove').

‡ Richard Vaughan, 'No-deal Brexit: Minister James Cleverly refuses to publish full details as public would "misunderstand"', *i*, 20 August 2019, https://inews.co.uk/news/politics/no-deal-brexit-operation-yellowhammer-government-refuse-full-publication-328801.

§ Mason, 'No 10 furious at leak of paper predicting shortages after no-deal Brexit'; 'The Operation Yellowhammer document was "deliberately leaked by a former minister in an attempt to influence discussions with EU leaders"', Boris Johnson Lies, 18 August 2019, https://boris-johnson-lies.com/the-operation-yellowhammer-document-was-deliberately-leaked-by-a-former.

¶ Mason, 'No 10 furious at leak of paper predicting shortages after no-deal Brexit'.

had retained a copy of the Yellowhammer document after leaving office and then leaked it, thereby committing an unethical and probably illegal act.

The result was that most of the following day's newspapers did not focus on the Yellowhammer disclosures about the dangers of a no-deal Brexit. Instead most turned Yellowhammer into a whodunnit – which of May's ministers had been the leaker? Most newspapers pointed the finger at Hammond, the former chancellor. Once again Downing Street was hard at work spreading lies and misinformation. The *Daily Mail* reported: 'A No 10 source blamed former frontbenchers led by Philip Hammond.'[*]

But no former minister could have been the leaker. The leaked document didn't even exist until Johnson had taken over.[†] The sorry story of the smear was therefore an example of how Boris Johnson's media operation operates through deceit, and how it relies on a compliant media to cooperate with that deceit – even when it knows the allegations are false.

---

[*] John Stevens and Larisa Brown, 'Storm over No Deal leak: No10 sources blame Philip Hammond for "revealing out-of-date doomsday dossier" detailing apocalyptic Brexit forecasts ahead of Boris Johnson's talks with EU', *MailOnline*, 18 August 2019, https://www.dailymail.co.uk/news/article-7369733/Storm-No-Deal-leak-No10-sources-blame-Philip-Hammond-date-doomsday-dossier.html.

[†] 'The Operation Yellowhammer document was "deliberately leaked by a former minister in an attempt to influence discussions with EU leaders"'.

There is an implicit deal. In return for access and information (much of it false), the political media was reporting a pro-government narrative. This means that Johnson's Downing Street can malign political opponents, lie about them and get away with it. But it can do this only because political journalists and editors allow it to. The anonymous Downing Street source who briefed the press about Yellowhammer was lying. It is notable how even *The Guardian*,* not a Tory newspaper, fell for this cynical and mendacious Downing Street ploy. Although now known to be a smear and a lie, it has never been corrected by any government spokesman.†

This technique vividly recalls the way US president Donald Trump has routinely been able to call on media allies, above all Fox News, to twist the political agenda away from his own lies and against his political enemies. But there is one difference between Johnson and Trump. There is a perverse kind of honesty – perhaps shamelessness

---

* Heather Stewart and Peter Walker, 'Yellowhammer: no-deal chaos fears as secret Brexit papers published', *The Guardian*, 12 September 2019, https://www.theguardian.com/politics/2019/sep/11/operation-yellowhammer-fears-no-deal-brexit-chaos-forced-to-publish-secret-papers.

† It would have been interesting and valuable to public life if Hammond had sued Boris Johnson for libel through his agent, the 'Number 10 source'. The justice system is not yet within Johnson's control. A court might have found for Hammond, and more important, ruled that all ministers are responsible for any anonymous briefing on their behalf. This ought to be in the Ministerial Code; it is a serious gap in responsibility. There is no hope of a correction under Johnson.

would be a better word – about the US president. Johnson kept himself in the background during the smearing of Philip Hammond. By contrast Trump seems to take pleasure in fabricating damaging stories about opponents and disseminating them personally on Twitter and elsewhere.*

Johnson stays for the most part above the fray, allowing members of his team to lie and cheat on his behalf, enabling him to maintain a cheery public demeanour.† As I have shown elsewhere in this book, Johnson's press briefers target civil servants as well as politicians, normally in an attempt to deflect blame from ministers.

To be fair to Johnson, he is not the first prime minister to abuse Downing Street in order to smear political opponents by spreading false stories. As I exposed fifteen years ago in my book *The Rise of Political Lying*, Tony Blair's government did something similar by spreading the false story that Britain's foreign intelligence agency, MI6, was investigating the Tory politician Chris Patten for leaking secrets while he was governor of Hong Kong.‡ But such episodes, while a disgraceful abuse of power, were relatively rare during

---

* I provide countless examples in *How Trump Thinks: His Tweets and the Birth of a New Political Language* (London: Head of Zeus, 2017).

† This two-faced strategy is not new. Chris Mullin's diary of his time as a New Labour minister reveals the advice Tony Blair gave his protégé David Miliband: 'Go around smiling at everyone and get other people to shoot them.' Chris Mullin, *A View from the Foothills* (London: Profile, 2009).

‡ Peter Oborne, *The Rise of Political Lying* (London: Free Press, 2005), pp. 52–4.

Blair's ten years as prime minister and the premierships of Brown, Cameron and May. Johnson, by contrast, had already adopted the tactic of cynically using the camouflage of Downing Street to spread lies and smears about opponents within weeks of taking office, and this kind of abuse soon became systemic during his premiership, as the account below shows.

TREACHERY

'No 10 probes Remain MPs' "foreign collusion"'. This huge banner headline dominated the front page of the *Mail on Sunday* on 29 September 2019.* Turn to page 2 and 'a senior No 10 source' was quoted in bold type: 'The government is working on extensive investigations into Dominic Grieve, Oliver Letwin and Hilary Benn and their involvement with foreign powers and the funding of their activities.' This story was granted huge prominence and followed up the next day by the *Daily Express*, *The Sun*, *The Times* and the alt-right news site Breitbart.

On the BBC's *Today* programme the following Tuesday, presenter Nick Robinson asked Boris Johnson about the investigation. Johnson gave credibility to the story when

---

* Glen Owen, 'No 10 probes Remain MPs' "foreign collusion" amid plot to allow John Bercow to send "surrender letter" to Brussels asking for a delay to Brexit', *MailOnline*, 29 September 2019, https://www.dailymail.co.uk/news/article-7516083/No-10-probes-MPs-foreign-collusion-amid-plot-John-Bercow-send-surrender-letter-Brussels.html.

he declared there were 'legitimate questions' to be asked of the MPs. But Robinson didn't ask the important question. Was there an investigation at all?

Something smelt fishy to me. First I rang Dominic Grieve. He told me he had not sought the help of any foreign government in drafting the so-called Benn Act, whose intention was to prevent the government from agreeing a no-deal Brexit.* He added that he was 'not in receipt of any sources of foreign funding'. Nor, he said, had he been contacted by Downing Street or anyone else about any investigation.

I then rang the Downing Street press office, and asked an official whether there was an investigation as stated in the *Mail on Sunday*. He told me categorically: 'No investigation.' A Cabinet Office spokesperson was even more categorical: 'There was never such an investigation.'

When I contacted the *Mail on Sunday*, it stood by its story: 'Two separate sources in Downing Street told us that officials in Number 10 were gathering evidence about allegations of foreign collusion by MPs opposed to a no-deal Brexit.' The paper's spokesperson also pointed out that Boris Johnson had given it credibility: 'When the prime minister was asked about our story on the BBC *Today* programme on 1 October he responded that there were "legitimate questions to be asked about the generation of this legislation"'.

*

---

* European Union (Withdrawal) (No. 2) Act 2019.

Glen Owen, the political editor behind the *Mail on Sunday* banner headline, is a senior and respected journalist. Though he correctly said that he wouldn't comment on his sources when I approached him, I am sure he didn't invent his 'senior No 10 source'. He will certainly have been briefed by powerful people who worked inside Downing Street. Nevertheless, his story was a fabrication. Not Glen Owen's fabrication. A fabrication made up by his Downing Street source.

In Johnson's Downing Street there were two kinds of truth. According to civil servants working inside Downing Street and the Cabinet Office, there was not and never had been an investigation into Benn, Letwin and Grieve. These civil servants were contractually bound to be politically impartial and had all signed up to the Nolan principles of selflessness and integrity.

But when Boris Johnson became prime minister he brought with him a group of political advisers into Downing Street led by his 'senior adviser', Dominic Cummings. I have no doubt that among this group were to be found the 'No 10 sources' who briefed journalists about the fictitious Downing Street investigation into the involvements of Hilary Benn and two other privy counsellors with foreign powers. For Cummings's team, there is no such thing as objective facts. For them truth is whatever a 'Downing Street source' tells a political journalist. It has become a weapon of power to suit the purposes of the moment.

But in ordinary language the Number 10 sources who

spoke to the *Mail on Sunday* were lying. As for the *Mail on Sunday* itself, it was disseminating false information to its 2.1 million readers.* This false information fitted like a glove with the dominant Downing Street narrative of the moment that the Benn Act was actually a 'surrender act' designed to thwart Brexit altogether.

Johnson's role in this unedifying affair was repellent. On the *Today* programme, the British prime minister could, and should, have taken the opportunity to tell the truth. Instead, he fuelled the smear with his statement that 'there are legitimate questions to be asked'.

As for the *Mail on Sunday*, it had entered into something like a conspiracy with Downing Street to mislead its readers into thinking that three honourable British politicians were conniving with a foreign power. The lie against Grieve, Letwin and Benn, like the one against Hammond, remains on the record. Benn is still a serving MP and was obliged to contend against the lie in his re-election campaign for his Leeds constituency.

It struck me that newspaper readers were entitled to be told about what Johnson's 10 Downing Street was like. So I made the way Boris Johnson was debauching Downing Street by using the power of his office to spread propaganda and fake news the subject of my weekly Saturday column for the *Daily Mail*. At around 5.15 p.m. (fairly late in the

---

* 'The Mail on Sunday', Newsworks, https://www.newsworks.org.uk/the-mail-on-sunday.

production cycle of a daily newspaper) I received a call from the editor, who indicated, with his customary exquisite good manners, that he would prefer I wrote about another subject. So I hammered out another column in record time.

Next I offered the piece to *The Spectator*, but the editor explained his refusal to publish on the reasonable grounds that the newspaper's political team had cultivated excellent insider sources and publishing my piece would invite charges of hypocrisy.

I had earlier approached Channel Four's *Dispatches*, which showed strong interest. The channel introduced me to a respected documentary production company. We went to the length of putting together a treatment for the film, after which I was called into a meeting in the Channel Four Horseferry Road HQ and told that the film was likely to go ahead subject to approval from the director of programmes when he returned from holiday next week. Whether because of the director of programmes, or for some other reason, I received a call a few days later saying that Channel Four was no longer interested. I then suggested to the TV production company that we might approach the BBC, but it said there was no chance it would be interested.

Finally, the website openDemocracy gave me a platform to write a detailed article about how, with the prime minister's encouragement, Downing Street or government sources have been spreading lies, misrepresentations, smears and falsehoods around Fleet Street and across the major TV channels.* I argued that senior British journalists are behaving as cheerleaders to the government. They are allowing the prime minister to get away with lies and dishonesty which they would never have permitted to his predecessor, Theresa May, let alone to Jeremy Corbyn, had he reached Number 10.

I also described how papers and media organisations yearn for privileged access and favourable treatment. And they are prepared to pay a price to get it. This price involves becoming a vital though subsidiary part of the government machine. It means turning their readers and viewers into dupes. This client journalism allows Downing Street to frame the story as it wants. Some allow themselves to be used as tools to smear the government's opponents. They say goodbye to the truth.

This article marked the end of my thirty-year-long career as a writer and broadcaster in the mainstream British press and media. I had been a regular presenter on Radio 4's *The Week in Westminster* for more than two decades. It ceased to use me, without explanation. I parted company on reasonably friendly terms with the *Daily Mail* after our disagreement.

The Guardian and the *Daily Mirror* both ran pieces from me about Tory lies during the election campaign. As the general election approached, I started my own website† listing

---

* Peter Oborne, 'British journalists have become part of Johnson's fake news machine', openDemocracy, 22 October 2019, https://www. opendemocracy.net/en/opendemocracyuk/british-journalists-have-become-part-of-johnsons-fake-news-machine/.

† https://boris-johnson-lies.com

the lies and falsehoods of Boris Johnson and his ministers. With so many to deal with, this was a time-consuming and expensive project, requiring a full-time team. We managed to keep it going until election day, and I frequently get urged to start it up again, but lack the time and resources.

The mainstream British press and media is to all intents and purposes barred to me. I continue to write for the website *Middle East Eye*, for openDemocracy and from time to time for the *British Journalism Review*. There I have concentrated on articles about journalists and reporters, primarily abroad, who live under the threat of torture, abduction and murder on account of their work.

In Britain that threat scarcely exists, though the case of Julian Assange gives grave cause for concern and (like Johnson's lies) has been ignored in the mainstream press.* It

---

* Assange, the founder of WikiLeaks, is currently serving time in Belmarsh jail and is fighting extradition to the United States on espionage charges. WikiLeaks is an international non-profit organisation that publishes news leaks and classified media provided by anonymous sources. As Human Rights Watch has pointed out, the British authorities have the power to prevent any US prosecution from eroding media freedom. Assange was arrested in April 2019 at the Ecuadorean embassy in London, where he had been staying since 2012. He sought asylum at the embassy to avoid extradition to Sweden on a 2010 rape allegation that he denied. An investigation into the rape allegation has now been dropped by Swedish prosecutors. See 'Julian Assange: A timeline of Wikileaks founder's case', BBC News, 19 November 2019, https://www. bbc.co.uk/news/world-europe-11949341; Peter Oborne, 'Julian Assange's case exposes British hypocrisy on press freedom', *Middle East Eye*, 5 May 2020, https://www.middleeasteye.net/opinion/ press-freedom-day-us-after-julian-assange-his-journalism.

takes infinitely less physical courage to expose government corruption and deceit in Britain than many other countries, though the financial consequences are significant. I am in my early sixties and drawing towards the end of my career. This made it easier to expose the rotten stench of mainstream British journalistic collaboration with Johnson's lies during the 2019 election.

Chapter Eight

THE CAPTURE OF THE CONSERVATIVE PARTY

'The business of government [is] not to inflame passion and give it new objects to feed on, but to inject into the activities of already passionate men an ingredient of moderation; to restrain, to deflate, to pacify and to reconcile.'

CONSERVATIVE PHILOSOPHER MICHAEL OAKESHOTT

'Whatever it takes'

MOTTO INSIDE JOHNSON'S DOWNING STREET

Fifteen years ago Boris Johnson hired me as political correspondent at *The Spectator* magazine. He was a joy to work for, a fine editor and a loyal colleague with the quickest mind I've ever encountered. Nothing needed explaining twice. While writing this book I've found myself trying to reconcile the person I knew then with the prime minister of Britain today.

We are talking about two different people. His magazine always stood up for the British institutions which Boris Johnson in power remorselessly attacks. His *Spectator* stood for the honest politics which he now subverts. While editor of *The Spectator*, Johnson eviscerated Tony Blair in the *Daily Telegraph* for the lies over weapons of mass destruction ahead of the Iraq War. 'At every stage, Blair upgrades hypothesis into fact,' mused Johnson, adding that 'he was utterly wrong to use such dishonest means of persuasion. He treated Parliament and the public with contempt.'* He might have been looking ahead to his own premiership. Johnson wanted Blair to be impeached.

Johnson's *Spectator* was politically eclectic and omnivorous, so much so that one or two critics said it was hard to discern where the paper stood on any subject. He had a sophisticated understanding of politics which disdained simple solutions. We would have long, lucid discussions of complex issues, either in weekly conference or at the famous *Spectator* lunches. Boris was sunny, liberal,

---

* Boris Johnson, 'Isn't it time to impeach Blair over Iraq?', *The Telegraph*, 26 August 2004, https://www.telegraph.co.uk/comment/personal-view/3610079/Isnt-it-time-to-impeach-Blair-over-Iraq.html. I also wrote about the attempts to impeach Blair in *The Spectator*: 'High crimes and misdemeanours', 28 August 2004, https://www.spectator.co.uk/article/high-crimes-and-misdemeanours.

optimistic. So how did the Johnson of *The Spectator* turn into today's prime minister?

What follows is no more than informed speculation, since no one can look into the soul of another human being. But here is my own attempt at reconciling the editor I worked for fifteen years ago with the prime minister in 10 Downing Street today.

I start with self-reproach. It bites away at me that I failed to pay attention to events which seem so significant with the benefit of hindsight. I was on the magazine when the Tory leader Michael Howard sacked Johnson as a junior party spokesman for lying.* I dismissed it as private business and, like almost everyone else (including Howard, who later supported Johnson's campaign for the leadership), forgot about it. We shouldn't have done.

Johnson's earlier misdemeanours didn't stop him becoming mayor of London. He ran London the identical way he earlier ran *The Spectator*, meaning that he was often absent and left the detail to others. But that didn't matter much because he chose capable deputies who did the hard work. The role of London mayor had been emasculated by Blair, its creator, in the justified fear that Ken Livingstone would win the first election for it. The mayor's main role was to become a public face and cheerleader for London. In that capacity, Johnson was a natural, and deserved to win his second term.

---

* As discussed in Chapter Four, p. 58.

This was the turning point for Johnson. His success as mayor stimulated his ambition to new heights. More importantly, his electoral triumph in a traditionally Labour-voting city meant that many Tories began to see him as someone who could help them win their seats.

By the time he stood down after eight years, Johnson had become a superstar who attracted crowds wherever he went (although his most-remembered achievement, the so-called Boris bikes, was actually a legacy from Ken Livingstone). Like Jacques Chirac after his term as mayor of Paris in 1995, he was poised for a final assault on national politics. Like Donald Trump after the 2016 presidential election, Johnson's electoral Midas touch encouraged his own party thereafter to give him a free pass to lie and cheat.

At this point David Cameron reached a decision which had huge consequences for himself, for the Conservative Party and for Britain. He offered Johnson a relatively senior cabinet role, hinting at defence secretary, but this was not enough to satisfy Johnson's ambition.* I guess Cameron did not fully understand Johnson, and underestimated his power across the country. Nor the effect losing Johnson to the leave campaign would have on the referendum.

This made Johnson's Brexit decision easy. If Cameron secured victory, Johnson could ponder a future as a

---

* Andrew Billen, 'David Cameron interview: Boris, Brexit and the referendum', *The Times*, 13 September 2019, https://thetimes.co.uk/article/david-cameron-interview-boris-johnson-brexit-and-the-referendum-9gkxqghv9.

middle-ranking Cabinet minister in a government dominated by his main rival. To be leader of the Brexit campaign opened up the potential of Downing Street. From Johnson's perspective, the result didn't matter. Even if he lost, he would still emerge strong enough to mount a formidable challenge to David Cameron. I suspect strongly that he hoped for a narrow defeat after an exciting campaign. That would have been the ideal platform for his leadership ambitions and spared him the immense complex and detailed tasks of taking responsibility for the United Kingdom's exit from the EU.

I'd guess (I stress that I can't be sure) that the future prime minister on balance agreed with Remain, but the real consideration was his career. He made a bargain. The Vote Leave campaign would propel him to Downing Street, and he would be their figurehead.

All politicians are in one sense actors in search of a scriptwriter. In Vote Leave's director, Dominic Cummings, Johnson found his scriptwriter. I now turn to what this meant for the Conservative Party.

Reverse Takeover

On the stock market a reverse takeover is defined as the purchase of a publicly owned company by a private group.[*]

---

[*] Marshall Hargrave, 'Reverse takeover (RTO)', Investopedia, 1 August 2020, https://www.investopedia.com/terms/r/reversetakeover.asp.

The private buyers do it because it provides a market listing without the lengthy, expensive and bureaucratic annoyance of an offer for sale. Just as significant, it can help them avoid public scrutiny.

In stock market terms, David Cameron's Conservative Party was ripe for takeover. Membership, which had reached a peak of 2.8 million after the Second World War, had collapsed – barely 100,000 and in free fall.* For each member in 2015 there had been twenty-eight in 1950. The world was changing and (like many famous British retail organisations) the party had not worked out how to move with it. It lacked identity, or even discernible purpose besides staying in office. In fairness, the Labour Party also had haemorrhaged active members over the same period. People had turned away from local political parties as an outlet for their social life, and looked more and more to single-issue campaigns for their political involvement. The membership of both parties became older and older, while the new recruits were all too often political obsessives who accelerated the flight of 'normal' people from local parties.

In spite of the membership collapse, the Conservative Party still had an old and resonant name. Legally it was the same organisation which had governed Britain for

---

* 'Partied out: political party membership', UK Parliament, https://www.parliament.uk/business/publications/research/olympic-britain/parliament-and-elections/partied-out/.

most of the previous 200 years, led by great leaders from Wellington and Disraeli to Churchill and Thatcher.* This gave it some of the characteristics of a corporate shell.

Financiers were alert to this and a new class of private donor began to emerge.† These donors were needed because the loss of millions of members had two malign effects. In the post-war era, the small subscriptions of a mass membership had sustained reasonably healthy party finances, particularly when parties still relied on volunteer doorstep campaigning in preference to national advertising. When those volunteers gradually disappeared, the party went into a vicious financial spiral at election time – forced into more expensive methods of reaching voters and with less and less regular income to pay for them.

A new model emerged. Party funds were provided by a new group of super-rich. Many of them were based

---

* It is still in Great Britain formally the Conservative and Unionist Party – a historic legacy of the Liberal Party split over home rule for Ireland in the late nineteenth century.

† All political parties follow certain rules, set out in the Political Parties, Elections and Referendums Act 2000, and overseen by the Electoral Commission. However, there is no limit on donations that a party can receive ('Giving a donation or loan', Electoral Commission, 30 July 2019, https://www.electoralcommission.org.uk/who-we-are-and-what-we-do/financial-reporting/donations-and-loans). It emerged in 2006 that to fund their 2005 general election campaigns, Labour was secretly loaned nearly £14 million and the Conservatives £16 million. This led to desire for reform and the 2006 Hayden inquiry into political donors; see 'Q&A: Political party funding', BBC News, 20 July 2007, http://news.bbc.co.uk/1/hi/uk_politics/6065322.stm.

offshore, secretive about the financial arrangements and obscure about their motives. Crucially, their money paid for the local party activists to be replaced by a superior cadre of political experts at the centre. Latterly, these created a new form of communication with voters through private polling, focus groups and, more recently, exploitation of social media so sophisticated that voters often do not even know that they are reading propaganda.* These novel techniques

---

* Online political advertising is largely unregulated in the UK and campaign material is not required by law to be truthful or factually accurate, or to say who is paying for it ('Online political ads are in urgent need of regulation', *Financial Times*, 1 November 2019, https://www.ft.com/content/e0a93d3c-fbd3-11e9-a354-36acbbb0d9b6). In 2019 the Electoral Reform Society, which campaigns for changes to the voting system, described it as being like the 'Wild West' and subject to rules stuck in the 'analogue age' (Michela Palese and Josiah Mortimer (eds), 'Reining in the Political "Wild West": Campaign Rules for the 21st Century', Electoral Reform Society, February 2019, https://www.electoral-reform.org.uk/wp-content/uploads/2019/02/Reining-in-the-Political-Wild-West-Campaign-Rules-for-the-21st-Century.pdf). A report from the Oxford Internet Institute published in 2019 found that the use of social media to manipulate public opinion is now a global problem (Samantha Bradshaw and Philip N. Howard, 'The Global Disinformation Order: 2019 Global Inventory of Organised Social Media Manipulation', Oxford Internet Institute, 2019, https://comprop.oii.ox.ac.uk/wp-content/uploads/sites/93/2019/09/CyberTroop-Report19.pdf).

In August 2020, the government published proposals for social media ads and videos to have to carry a 'digital imprint' showing who has created them so voters can judge their credibility ('Transparency in digital campaigning: technical consultation on digital imprints', Gov.uk, 12 August 2020, https://www.gov.uk/government/consultations/transparency-in-digital-campaigning-technical-consultation-on-digital-imprints). This has been called the 'bare minimum' by some critics; see 'Online political campaigning "to be

opened the opportunity for new forms of lying, political engineering and deceit.

In return for their money, these donors gained access to power. Some wanted material rewards in the shape of profitable planning consents, or changes to the law which helped their business. Others purchased social status in the form of knighthoods and peerages. The most significant category wanted to impose their ideological agenda. There was a special group of people whose money came from Russia trying to legitimise if not actually launder it and buy influence and status in Britain.

To be fair, neither David Cameron nor Boris Johnson started this. Politics was hollowing out before either arrived on the scene.[*] Nor was it a uniquely Conservative phenomenon. New Labour did the same thing, and for similar reasons, deliberately using business donors to marginalise the trade unions. But this sombre background does explain why a degraded Conservative Party was so vulnerable for takeover. Johnson became the instrument. Upon his becoming prime minister, Downing Street was at once captured by Vote Leave. This included his senior adviser Dominic Cummings and the Downing Street director of communications, Lee

---

more transparent"', BBC News, 12 August 2020, https://www.bbc.co.uk/news/uk-politics-53741171.

[*] Colin Crouch, 'Coping with Post-Democracy', Fabian Society, 2000, https://www.fabians.org.uk/wp-content/uploads/2012/07/Post-Democracy.pdf.

Cain, with heavyweight political support from Michael Gove and Priti Patel.

Vote Leave was a tiny organisation with no members, a handful of executives and a powerful donor base. This group despised the Conservative Party and hated British institutions. Cummings denounced non-compliant MPs as 'narcissist-delusional',[*] and idly speculated about 'bombing Parliament'.[†] He was in contempt of Parliament even before being appointed.[‡] The Cabinet became irrelevant. Whereas Johnson had chosen a serious team of people round him as mayor of London, now only loyalty counted, meaning that the Cabinet became a collection of non entities or worse.

Cummings and Johnson are creatures of big money – a point persistently ignored by Britain's client political press. 'After this meeting,' Cummings reportedly told a meeting of special advisers, 'I'm going to go and meet billionaire hedge fund managers and get a giant pot of cash from them.'[§]

---

[*] Sam Coates, 'Leave campaign chief Dominic Cummings in tirade at "narcissist-delusional" Brexiteers', *The Times*, 27 March 2019, https://www.thetimes.co.uk/article/leave-campaign-chief-dominic-cummings-in-tirade-at-narcissist-delusional-brexiteers-k9wkm7tmc.

[†] Jonathan Heawood, 'Monster or guru? What Dominic Cummings' blog tells us about him', *The Guardian*, 15 August 2019, https://www.theguardian.com/politics/2019/aug/15/dominic-cummings-blog-political-values.

[‡] Rajeev Syal and agencies, 'Dominic Cummings found in contempt of parliament', *The Guardian*, 27 March 2019, https://www.theguardian.com/politics/2019/mar/27/commons-report-rules-dominic-cummings-in-contempt-of-parliament.

[§] Tim Shipman, 'Climb aboard for Boris Johnson's white-knuckle

'Whatever it takes' became the motto in Downing Street – a term reminiscent of Malcolm X's use of the phrase 'by any means necessary' when he rejected the non-violence of Martin Luther King.[*] In this context, that means: Lie. Cheat. Bully. Threaten. Independent-minded Tory MPs were driven out.[†] Loyalty became the only criterion for promotion. The Conservative Party turned into a Vote Leave sect.

It's important to recognise that if the Tories had failed to deliver Brexit – as many MPs from all sides hoped – the party would have been in terrible trouble. The Vote Leave stance – against Parliament and the civil service, both widely seen by Leavers as thwarting Brexit – was beyond doubt supported by many voters. But responsible prime ministers try to temper their supporters' extremes. Boris Johnson fanned the flames and exploited divisions.

Conservatives used to be careful students of history. They knew that men and women are frail, imperfect,

---

general election ride', *Sunday Times*, 25 August 2019, https://www.thetimes.co.uk/article/climb-aboard-for-boris-johnsons-white-knuckle-general-election-ride-927t9nvpq.

[*] 'Malcolm X: "By any means necessary"', *Washington Post*, 20 February 2015, https://www.washingtonpost.com/video/national/malcolm-xs-by-any-means-necessary-speech/2015/02/20/16fecd00-b955-11e4-bc30-a4e75503948a_video.html.

[†] Alix Culbertson and Rebecca Taylor, 'Tory rebels: The MPs who were sacked or resigned over no-deal Brexit', Sky News, 9 September 2019, https://news.sky.com/story/tory-rebels-the-mps-who-were-sacked-or-resigned-over-no-deal-brexit-11804764.

corruptible and, at times, capable of great evil. That explains why they always paid such attention to the importance of institutions which, as Edmund Burke explained, embody wisdoms and truths which are beyond the comprehension of individual minds. Vote Leave is destroying these institutions.

Michael Oakeshott, the greatest Conservative thinker of the twentieth century, noted that there was no Conservative ideology. Instead, there was a Conservative disposition which 'understands it to be the business of government not to inflame passion and give it new objects to feed on, but to inject into the activities of already passionate men an ingredient of moderation; to restrain, to deflate, to pacify and to reconcile'.* Vote Leave and Johnson systematically seek to create division and culture wars, something else they have in common with Donald Trump. Like Trump, they have been helped by a ruling class which made significant bodies of voters feel ignored and despised. Like him, they promised these voters power and revenge. Take Back Control was actually a much better slogan than Trump's Make America Great Again. It was multi-layered in its appeal, promising to Take Back Control not only from the remote EU but from all those in Britain whom disenchanted voters blamed for their unsatisfactory lives.

---

* Richard Cockett, 'Oakeshott's lessons for a warring party', *Standpoint*, 30 May 2019, https://standpointmag.co.uk/oakeshotts-lessons-for-a-warring-party/.

A New Epistemology

Let's now take a second look at the Boris Johnson who was editor of *The Spectator* fifteen years ago. The magazine he edited was the embodiment of traditional Conservatism, with its respect for institutions and understanding of due process. It was founded at roughly the same time as the Tory Party in the aftermath of the French Revolution and in response to the Parliamentary Reform agitation in Britain.* Like the Tory Party, it emerged as a defender of institutions and due process – church, monarchy, Parliament, rule of law – against abstraction, ideology and ultimately political violence.

When he joined Vote Leave Johnson chucked this kind of Conservatism aside. Not only was Vote Leave an anti-establishment project, but at its heart was a readiness to place the end before the means – in other words neglect of due process, readiness to mislead, and Leninist obsession with ideological rectitude. Cummings, who had spent a few years in Russia after leaving university, was fascinated by the brilliant communist propagandist Willi Münzenberg, a close friend of Lenin who became one of the Bolsheviks' crucial assets in Europe after the revolution.†

---

* The Conservative Party was founded around 1834. *The Spectator* was founded in 1828.

† See Babette Gross, *Willi Münzenberg: A Political Biography*, tr. Marian Jackson (East Lansing: Michigan State University Press, 1974).

Münzenberg used the phrase 'lying for the truth'.* For him truth was the communist cause. According to the writer Stephen Koch, Münzenberg 'wanted to instil the feeling like a truth of nature, that seriously to criticise or challenge Soviet policy was the unfailing mark of a bad, bigoted, and probably stupid person, while support was equally infallible proof of a forward-looking mind committed to all that was best for humanity and marked by an uplifting refinement of sensibility'.†

So it was with Cummings's Vote Leave. Lacking a moral system of his own, Johnson adapted easily to this new epistemology. It gave him the freedom to make any statement he liked. This may help explain the epidemic of lying inside Boris Johnson's Downing Street. This assault on truth was part of a fundamental assault on the values and institutions that had governed Britain for centuries. In the next chapter I examine the consequences.

---

* Stephen Koch, 'Lying for the truth: Münzenberg and the Comintern', *New Criterion*, November 1993, pp. 16–35, https://newcriterion.com/issues/1993/11/lying-for-the-truth-manzenberg-and-the-comintern.
† Ibid.

Chapter Nine

CONCLUSION

'The people of England are now renowned, all over the world, for their great virtue and discipline; and yet suffer an idiot, without courage, without sense, nay, without ambition, to have dominion in a country of liberty.'

SIR HENRY VANE

The unhappy fact that a fabricator and cheat controls the destiny of Britain raises deep, troublesome questions that go way beyond the moral character of Boris Johnson. What happened to the British? How on earth did we vote for him? These questions have nagged away at me while I have been writing this book.

One immediate answer is to look at the quality of his opponents, first in the Conservative Party leadership contest and then in the general election of 2019. In the leadership contest, only one contender, the relatively unknown and politically exotic Rory Stewart, carried the war to Johnson, particularly over Brexit. When he was eliminated, in a ballot of Conservative MPs alone, none of the other candidates attacked Johnson's fundamental fitness to be the party leader and prime minister.

Then Johnson had the good luck to be faced by Jeremy Corbyn – in a general election gifted to him by Corbyn's decision to allow him to hold it at all.

Johnson was certainly very lucky in his opponents. But it remains extraordinary that he was able to reach the pinnacle of British politics after behaviours and evidence of character defects which would have scuppered the ambitions of earlier politicians. How did this happen?

After all, British politics has always produced its fair share of cheats and fabricators. But barriers stood in their way, meaning they got found out. This means the fact that Boris Johnson made it into 10 Downing Street ultimately tells us much more about the rest of us than about him.

Here's my answer. The prime minister rose to the top at the end of a long period of British peace and prosperity following the end of the Second World War. During this time, a new generation emerged which had never known the suffering, danger and sacrifice of war. We took political stability, something which history shows is rare and precious, for granted.

Boris Johnson at his best is a superlative entertainer,

funny, charming, amiable. He is wonderfully gifted at playing Bertie Wooster while others pursue on his behalf the agenda of Roderick Spode. He is the perfect leader for a country where you can say or do anything without suffering the consequences.

It is suggestive to contrast Johnson's escalator to the top – private school, Eton, Oxford University, the *Daily Telegraph* and the Conservative Party – with Angela Merkel in communist East Germany, repressed and deprived. Unlike Johnson, Merkel is a serious person running a serious country. She had to be, having been raised in a hardline communist state where words and actions had to be measured with intense care. Students of her career also point to her scientific background as the key to her success.*

Facts matter to her because theories only carry weight if the evidence is rigorously inspected. A *New Yorker* profile written six years ago put this neatly: 'Trained to see the invisible world in terms of particles and waves, Merkel learned to approach problems methodically, drawing comparisons, running scenarios, weighing risks, anticipating reactions, and then, even after making a decision, letting it sit for a while before acting.'†

---

* George Packer, 'The quiet German: the astonishing rise of Angela Merkel, the most powerful woman in the world', *New Yorker*, 1 December 2014, https://www.newyorker.com/magazine/2014/12/01/quiet-german.

† Ibid.

Moreover, she represented a country which had thought with humility and acute intelligence about how to avoid a repeat of the horror of the twentieth century. For Angela Merkel, freedom of movement, stable institutions and democracy were in themselves miracles, not something to be taken for granted. They needed protection.

Britain and the United States took the opposite course. As the current century began, both countries turned their backs on the deep, hard-won institutional wisdom which enabled them to survive two great twentieth-century wars and the long struggle against the Soviet Union which followed. We embraced the trivial above the serious, the showy rather than the solid, while rejecting the rule of law and mocking domestic and international institutions.* Britain and America debauched their magnificent democratic legacy rather than protecting it.

Johnson has become the master of a new discourse that was manufactured for a weightless world where leaders depend on facts that have either been twisted beyond recognition or do not even exist. In this world, argument descends into sloganeering. These slogans can feel legitimate because they make political arguments simple. For

---

* The 2003 invasion of Iraq is the most notorious example of how Britain and America were becoming increasingly hostile to the rule of law. It is a fundamental principle of international law that states are prohibited from using force except in self-defence or unless its use is authorised by the Security Council under Chapter VII of the UN charter. Neither of these conditions applied ahead of the Iraq invasion.

example, terms like 'Get Brexit Done' – which helped Johnson's Conservatives to win the 2019 election – come over as lucid, unambiguous and easy to understand. But this impression is deceptive. The moment you attempt to grapple with them you realise they are a minefield of contradictions, lies and unworkable assumptions.

Political argument is always complicated and cannot readily be compressed into three words. These endlessly repeated slogans are about selling product rather than actual political discussion. This should surprise nobody because three-word slogans were one of the mass persuasion techniques developed by the advertising industry at the start of the twentieth century. Advertising rejects nuance and complexity. There is no room for truth in the world of the stark assertion and the hard sell. It thrives on simplification and the bare, unsubstantiated association of a product with personal success and happiness.

In the previous chapter, I looked back at the healthy politics of the post-war era. Along with mass party membership, the most striking fact was the continuity of style and content in all types of political language, whether official documents, popular journalism, political speeches and party manifestos.* It is a paradox that at a time of rigid

---

* See Colin Crouch's brilliant Fabian Society pamphlet 'Coping with Post-Democracy': 'If one looks back to the different forms of political discussion in the inter- and post-war decades one is surprised at the relative similarity of language and style in government documents, serious journalism, popular journalism, party manifestos and

class divides, when only a small fraction of men (and a tiny number of women) attended university, we enjoyed a common language which made us part of the same national discourse. That has all gone. I now turn to what has replaced it.

ROUSSEAU VS MONTESQUIEU

On the one hand we have private conversations within the elite. The ruminations of Dominic Cummings, Johnson's senior adviser, are full of long words and references which are inaccessible to all but the adept. Here's an example taken more or less at random from Cummings's blog:

> There is very powerful feedback between: a) creating dynamic tools to see complex systems deeper (to see inside, see across time, and see across possibilities), thus making it easier to work with reliable knowledge and interactive quantitative models, semi-automating error-correction etc, and b) the potential for big improvements in the performance of political and government decision-making.*

---

politicians' public speeches.' Colin Crouch, 'Coping with Post-Democracy', Fabian Society, 2000, p. 9, https://www.fabians.org.uk/wp-content/uploads/2012/07/Post-Democracy.pdf.

* 'On the referendum #33: High performance government, "cognitive technologies", Michael Nielsen, Bret Victor, & "Seeing Rooms"', Dominic Cummings's Blog, 26 June 2019, https://dominiccummings.com/2019/06/26/on-the-referendum-33-high-performance-government-cognitive-technologies-michael-nielsen-bret-victor-seeing-rooms/.

Cummings's blog is almost unreadable, endlessly spewing out managerial babble of this kind, and very scanty with actual policy proposals for government. The only one I could discover on an admittedly hurried reading was a call for a manned lunar base.

On the other hand, we have conversations between the elite and the people. Note that Cummings drops this elevated chat when addressing voters or telling others how to do so. Their language then becomes superficially more direct and empathetic, but on deeper examination it reveals itself as a patronising and manipulative discourse which has nothing truly in common with the language used by the person in the street – or even everyday practical politics.*

Indeed, Cummings's verbless formulations are constructed to be out of reach of either of these modes of true democratic engagement.† There are arresting comparisons to be made between the way the power elite engages with voters today and pre-modern political discourse, before the emergence of democratic structures and mass parties. The contemporary version is worse, because it is so cynical, knowing and dishonest. At least the eighteenth-century

---

* Notice the way that Johnson uses the term 'kids' rather than 'children', and addresses voters as 'folks'. People live in 'homes' and not 'houses'. He is not alone in this; see Peter Oborne and Anne Williams, 'The new language of political narcissism', *Standpoint*, 23 February 2015, https://standpointmag.co.uk/features-march-15-language-of-political-narcissism-peter-oborne/.

† Crouch, 'Coping with Post-Democracy', p. 9.

French monarchy and nobility sincerely believed that they were entitled by divine right to rule the masses. So a world has evolved in which politics is divided between the ruler and the ruled, the fixer and the fixed. Underlying all of this is a profound arrogance and brutal contempt for voters and indeed for the structures of democracy itself.*

Politicians address individual people in this familiar tone in order to simulate a personal connection that does not exist. At the heart of the new politics is the nightmare assumption that emotion is more important than thought. This dangerous insight lies at the heart of the politics of Johnson and Trump.

Alternatives were canvassed as the French monarchy lost its way in the eighteenth century. The political scientist Charles Montesquieu (an admirer of the British constitution) advocated separation of powers between parliament, the judiciary and executive.† He held that this would avert both

---

* It is striking that the two senior Conservative politicians to whom straightforward political discussion came most naturally, the former chancellor Kenneth Clarke and Rory Stewart, were expelled from the party after Johnson became prime minister. Clarke and Stewart, along with nineteen other Conservative MPs, had the whip removed on 4 September 2019 for rebelling against the government in a bid to avoid a no-deal Brexit. 'Brexit showdown: Who were Tory rebels who defied Boris Johnson?', BBC News, 5 September 2019, https://www.bbc.co.uk/news/uk-politics-49563357.

† Montesquieu's ideas were particularly influential in the United States. One of the founding fathers, James Madison, said: 'The accumulation of all powers, legislative, executive, and judiciary, in the same hands, whether of one, a few, or many, and whether hereditary, selfappointed [sic], or elective, may justly be pronounced the very definition of tyranny' (James Madison, *The Federalist Papers*, No. 47).

the despotism of the Bourbon monarchs and the tyranny of democracy, thus maintaining order while securing liberty.

These ideas were challenged by the philosopher Jean-Jacques Rousseau, who argued that humanity is naturally virtuous but turned vicious thanks to the corrupting influence of society: 'God makes all things good; man meddles with them and they become evil.'* Rousseau advocated the abolition of institutions and their replacement by direct democracy, expressed through what he called the general will. He thought this would preserve man's natural virtue, because it was the only way human beings could give their consent to being governed.

In France, Rousseau won out with the French Revolution. In Britain and the United States, Rousseau lost to Montesquieu. The political systems of both countries were constructed to stifle anything resembling Rousseau's general will. Popular opinion was held to be fickle, ignorant and combustible.

Democracy has therefore been constrained by second chambers, revising procedures, a permanent civil service, judges and other prophylactics against the untrammelled operation of the popular will. Formal checks on popular sovereignty were especially important in the early United States, particularly an unelected Senate (which lasted over a hundred years) and the Electoral College to avoid direct election of the

---

* Jean-Jacques Rousseau, *Emile* (1762). He said something similar in a more famous phrase: 'Man is born free but is everywhere in chains' (*The Social Contract* (1762)).

president, which still bedevils American elections and threatens to engender the collapse of the United States as a polity.

This limited form of democratic government – called 'liberal democracy' or sometimes 'representative democracy' – has given rise to resentment, especially in the United States. Its agents are seen (sometimes with justice) as a vested interest, which is why Donald Trump won votes when he promised to 'drain the swamp'. (Promises unkept: Trump's administration, like Johnson's, handsomely rewarded its donors.)

The first anti-establishment candidate to crash the system was the war hero Andrew Jackson on a programme of hostility to federal power, support for white nationalism and entrenched opposition to the abolition of slavery.* It's no coincidence that one of Donald Trump's first acts as president was to visit Jackson's home in Tennessee. After Jackson's death, the 'Know Nothing Party' became the first movement to make systematic use of conspiracy theories, peddling fake Catholic plots to subvert the American working man through Irish whiskey, German lager and cheap migrant labour. At its peak, the Know-Nothings had over a hundred congressmen and eight state governors. Later 'populist' movements counted on ferocious press support. Donald Trump's favourite film, Orson Welles's *Citizen Kane*, is based on the tycoon William Randolph Hearst, whose press empire exploited alarm about immigration

---

* H. W. Brands, *Andrew Jackson: His Life and Times* (New York: Anchor, 2006).

to position itself as champion of the forgotten American working class against the corrupt Washington elite.

Hearst foreshadowed Rupert Murdoch, whose outlets likewise blur the boundary between news and entertainment, spreading lies about immigrants while targeting vulnerable minorities and waging war against liberal institutions. Through Fox News, Murdoch provided a backbone of support for Trump, while in Britain his newspapers propelled Boris Johnson to power. Murdoch is therefore one of the most powerful links between Johnson and Trump. Even more important than Murdoch, however, is that the British prime minister and the American president are driven by a hauntingly similar political philosophy.

The Tribal Epistemology of Johnson and Trump

It's not immediately obvious that either leader has a philosophy at all, so this takes a little explanation with some help from the Stanford University philosopher Thomas Sowell. In his masterly *A Conflict of Visions* Sowell showed that conservatives and progressives have long had a conflicting conception of human nature.*

---

* What Sowell called the 'constrained vision' sees human nature as selfish and unchanging. In sharp contrast the 'unconstrained vision' sees human nature as benign and perfectible. Thomas Sowell, *A Conflict of Visions* (New York: William Morrow, 1987).

Conservatives, as careful students of history, sense that men and women are frail, imperfect, corruptible and capable of great evil. That is why conservatives have paid special attention to the importance of institutions: established church, parliament, monarchy, the law courts, universities, the regimental tradition and so on. They understand that these institutions embody wisdoms and truths which are beyond the comprehension of individual minds, however clever. Edmund Burke, born in Ireland and – though by trade a journalist and politician – the nearest thing we have to a conservative philosopher, declared: 'I feel an insuperable reluctance in giving my hand to destroy any established institution of government, upon a theory, however plausible it may be.'

The doctrine of the frailty of man also explains the stress laid by conservatives on apparently minor matters – due process, proper note taking, grammar, good manners and, above all, truth telling. Conservatives sense that human imperfection means that plans for far-reaching change are likely to go wrong. So they prefer to concentrate on smaller matters over which we have direct control.

Progressives tend to see human nature in the opposite way. They believe that institutions frustrate progress because they obstruct self-expression. They think that sincerity – the desire to do the right thing – is much more important than a stuffy insistence on procedure. The end justifies the means. To quote the Viennese political economist J. A. Schumpeter: 'The first thing a man will do for his ideals is lie.'*

I accept that this is an oversimplification, and that progressives have frequently been on the side of legality in the defence of their values against right-wing power, as for example when they rallied opinion for the Spanish Republic, the lawful elected government of Spain, against the rebel generals. But I think it fair to say that progressives, unlike conservatives, see little value in institutions for their own sake. They judge them by their use in furthering progressive goals.

It is mesmerising that both Johnson and Trump, though leaders of the Tory and Republican parties respectively, embody progressive rather than conservative insights about human nature. They are with Rousseau and the French Revolution rather than Montesquieu and the American Constitution. They think the end justifies the means. They wage permanent war on institutions, despise due process and feel enfranchised to fabricate and twist the truth. They reject the Burkeian wisdom that we need to support institutions and observe due process to protect society against the weakness of humanity.

But they wage this war from the right and not the left. I showed in Chapter Three that while Bill Clinton and Tony Blair were both liars, they believed that, as progressive

---

* Joseph A. Schumpeter, *History of Economic Analysis* (London: Routledge, [1945] 1997), p. 43.

leaders, their lying was sanctioned because it was for the greater good. Trump and Johnson are different. Neither lies out of idealism. Both leaders prey on the dark side of human nature. Both combine right-wing political instincts with progressive methods.

This is rare in the history of conservative politics, but not unknown. Bertrand Russell wrote of Rousseau's idea of the general will, and its intolerance for minorities, in 1946: 'Its first fruits in practice were the reign of Robespierre; the dictatorships of Russia and Germany (especially the latter) are the outcome of Rousseau's teaching.'*

History does not repeat itself, but it is wise to pay attention to its lessons. Trump and Johnson lie for power, to get their way, to save their skins, sometimes, one feels, for the sheer hell of it. Trump relies on his standing as the anti-establishment outsider who can rely on the common man against enemies, real and imaginary, while Johnson often conducts himself as if he believes the Brexit referendum of June 2016 has given him a political legitimacy to trash British institutions like Parliament, the Supreme Court and the BBC.

For both the prime minister and the president, truth has become a weapon which can be reshaped, cancelled or deployed according to the needs of the moment. This means they are redefining the idea of truth that has lain

---

* Bertrand Russell, *History of Western Philosophy* (London: George Allen & Unwin, 1946), p. 674.

at the heart of public discourse in Britain and the United States for the last 250 years. This is the notion that truth is something we can share. Instead, the American president and the British prime minister are transferring truth from public into private hands. This is, in some ways, similar to the privatisation of water or electricity companies. Truth falls into the hands of a new and unaccountable set of owners. It can be bought and sold by shareholders, poisoned and polluted and turned into an instrument of state or private power.

Above all, however, this means ditching the idea of an outside verifiable reality, one of the central ideas of the Anglo-American school of empirical philosophy. In fact, it means denying the existence of independent reality at all and abolishing what President Obama called the 'common baseline of facts'.*

Social anthropologists have a term for this: tribal epistemology.† In a profound reshaping of the public domain, the long-accepted distinction between truth and falsehood is replaced by truth and error. In the words of the American journalist David Roberts: 'Information is evaluated not on conformity to common standards of evidence or

---

* Alana Abramson, '"We don't share a common baseline of facts." Barack Obama reflects on divisiveness in politics', *Time*, 12 January 2018, https://time.com/5099521/barack-obama-david-letterman-interview/.

† Helmut Wautischer, *Tribal Epistemologies: Essays in the Philosophy of Anthropology* (Abingdon: Routledge, [1998] 2018).

correspondence to a common understanding of the world, but on whether it supports the tribe's values and goals and is vouchsafed by tribal leaders. "Good for our side" and "true" begin to blur into one.'*

There is nothing new about this kind of attitude. Recalling his experiences in the Spanish Civil War, George Orwell wrote: 'But what impressed me then, and has impressed me ever since, is that atrocities are believed in or disbelieved in solely on grounds of political predilection. Everyone believes in the atrocities of the enemy and disbelieves in those of his own side, without ever bothering to examine the evidence.'† This epistemology is natural in a civil war. But it is incompatible with democracy. It removes the possibility of fair-minded argument. The other side can only be wrong and must be shouted down or suppressed.

This attitude helps explain why President Trump and Prime Minister Johnson get away with so many lies. Their supporters assume that whatever they say is true, and whatever their opponents say is false. There has always been a strong element of this in even democratic discourse, but it's got much worse. The rise of social media

---

* David Roberts, 'Donald Trump and the rise of tribal epistemology', *Vox*, 19 May 2017, https://www.vox.com/policy-and-politics/2017/3/22/14762030/donald-trump-tribal-epistemology.

† George Orwell, 'Looking Back on the Spanish War' (1942), Orwell Foundation, https://www.orwellfoundation.com/the-orwell-foundation/orwell/essays-and-other-works/looking-back-on-the-spanish-war/.

has not helped. When the internet got going twenty-five years ago there was reason to hope that it would lead to a more diverse and generous political discourse. We now know that it can discourage nuance, create isolated communities and spread hatred and bigotry, and that it is open to manipulation.*

We are slowly learning about the consequences. If defeated in an election, the other side is expected to acquiesce in everything the victors do, and silence their belief that the victors are mistaken. We are losing that common domain where rival groups can come together peacefully and in good faith. Democracy can function only when all sides agree some common basis of truth and how to establish it.

HOW TO FIGHT BACK

The British prime minister has repeatedly lied. About economic policy, about Brexit, about trade, about borders, about the Covid pandemic. He has lied to voters,

---

* In his 2019 book *This Is Not Propaganda*, Peter Pomerantsev, one of the most eloquent analysts of the relationship between social media and politics, speaks of 'populism as strategy' where an 'enemy' is manufactured to help unite support behind a political project. 'Facts become secondary in this logic,' writes Pomerantsev. 'After all, you are not trying to win an evidence-driven debate about ideological concepts in a public sphere; your aim is to seal in your audience behind a verbal wall' (Peter Pomerantsev, *This Is Not Propaganda: Adventures in the War against Reality* (London: Faber & Faber, 2019), p. 209).

to ministers, to journalists, to Parliament. He has lied to adults. He has lied to children.*

Nobody would tolerate this level of deceit in a friend, a colleague, an employer or a spouse. Yet Johnson's lying has been facilitated and, in many cases, actively defended, by MPs, the Conservative Party itself, allies in the press – and by millions of voters. Not only does Boris Johnson tell lies but his government has encouraged a culture of lying, in which lies are normal and their practitioners rewarded. This culture is corroding the British state.

Here are some ways we can all fight back against it.

One: Parliament must once again take lying seriously. I am sending this book to the speaker of the House of Commons, Lindsay Hoyle, and to the Lord Speaker, Norman Fowler. I will urge both to take action against any government statements which mislead their respective Houses, and in particular to demand that these be corrected within one week by a written ministerial statement in their respective Hansards, within a special space for ministerial corrections. Sometimes statements made in good faith are corrected on the basis of more up-to-date

---

* Johnson gave a speech to schoolchildren at Castle Rock School in Leicestershire on 26 August 2020 where he blamed a 'mutant algorithm' for the exam results crisis, despite having described the results as 'dependable' and 'robust' just days before. Heather Stewart, 'Boris Johnson blames "mutant algorithm" for exams fiasco', *The Guardian*, 26 August 2020, https://www.theguardian.com/politics/2020/aug/26/boris-johnson-blames-mutant-algorithm-for-exams-fiasco.

information. That would be shown on the minister's correction.

Crucially, this would enable the public to assume that without such an indication the original statement was made in bad faith. Whoever made it would be named and shamed. That would be a useful deterrent. If you agree with this idea, please write to both Speakers to support it.

Two: if you have a Conservative MP, as soon as you become aware of a government lie, ask him or her to demand its retraction and correction. If you get a negative or weak reply, ask your local media to name and shame the MP.

Three: if you are a public servant and you are asked to prepare or abet a government lie, ask for a written order from your superior. Send a copy of this to your permanent secretary or other chief of your organisation and whoever is appointed to listen to staff concerned about acting unethically. (Every public organisation has one, although yours may be hard to find.)

Four: this is unlikely, but if you are directly attacked in a government lie from a ministerial source, sue the minister concerned. Sue Boris Johnson himself if the lie comes from Number 10, as so many do. If you know anyone in this position, ask him or her to do the same. Serving a writ for defamation on the minister, especially Boris Johnson, in a public place would be a valuable demonstration that ministers should take responsibility for their underlings.

Five: I have not mentioned the assault by Boris Johnson and his ministers on the judiciary. So far this has been verbal rather than practical, and was very well set out by the popular Secret Barrister in *The Guardian*.* A key message in all the attacks, particularly over the Brexit decisions, is that the judges are frustrating the will of the people. This is a coded attack on Parliament as well as the judiciary, since the latter were only enforcing the law as passed by Parliament. Again, you might care to put pressure on your MP if he or she is a Conservative. Ask him or her to commit to opposing any government which a) restrains the public from seeking to make the government obey the law; b) limits their chance of finding an affordable lawyer to do this for them; c) limits the power of the judiciary to make the government comply with the law. Again, name and shame any MP who gives a poor reply. It is worth asking Conservative peers to make the same commitment if you know any, since the House of Lords (stuffed with senior lawyers) is likely to be a better source of resistance.

Six: if you take any of these initiatives, you must inform the Committee on Standards in Public Life. We still have one, although it is a sleeping giant. The chairman is Lord Evans of Weardale, the former chief of the domestic intelligence service MI5. He has been slow to wake up.

---

* Secret Barrister, 'Against the law: why judges are under attack, by the Secret Barrister', *The Guardian*, 22 August 2020, https://www.theguardian.com/books/2020/aug/22/against-the-law-why-judges-are-under-attack-by-the-secret-barrister.

Seven: insist that our newspapers and media care about the truth. Complain if they repeat the prime minister's many lies. Demand that they challenge the prime minister when he lies. This is important because many of us in media as well as politics were part of this destruction of the public space. We still are. There are exceptions, but few and isolated. That is because the problem is not personal. We have on our hands a *structural* fascination with the short-term, the transient and destructive. We in the media have built up charlatans and we have abandoned the virtues of honesty, integrity, self-sacrifice and a sense of duty. We have been parochial twice over: first, in our failure to pay serious attention to the rest of the world; second, in our neglect of the lessons of our own history. We have treated politics as a game.

The adulation of Boris Johnson and Donald Trump, media superstars in politics, is the most obvious manifestation of this collective act of betrayal. But ultimately Johnson and Trump are only the symptom and not the cause. It is time to stand and fight for decency, tolerance, truth, and the freedom which comes with it. Serious times of suffering, tragedy and hardship now lie ahead.

Postscript

Donald Trump's relatively narrow defeat in the 2020 US election led to a final deluge of lies from the White House. The outgoing president refused to concede defeat long after the result became obvious, and for several weeks publicly entertained conspiracy theories that Joe Biden's victory was fraudulent.[*]

Trump deployed the state apparatus to substantiate these wild and combustible claims. Trump's attorney general, William Barr, authorised an official investigation into supposed voting irregularities.[†] Meanwhile, Secretary of State

---

[*] Glenn Kessler and Salvador Rizzo, 'President Trump's false claims of vote fraud: A chronology', *Washington Post*, 5 November 2020, https://www.washingtonpost.com/politics/2020/11/05/president-trumps-false-claims-vote-fraud-chronology/.

[†] Kadhim Shubber, 'US attorney-general authorizes probes into possible election fraud', *Financial Times*, 10 November 2020, https://www.ft.com/content/231a93c2-62d1-4f8f-9f49-35b235af44fe.

Mike Pompeo talked about 'a smooth transition to a second Trump administration'.*

Britain would normally have condemned this conduct. Despite being given opportunities to do so, neither Boris Johnson, nor his foreign secretary Dominic Raab, challenged Trump's account of events.†

More than that Boris Johnson was slow to congratulate Joe Biden, and when he finally did so a mistake meant the words 'Trump' and 'second term' could faintly be seen in the prime minister's message of congratulations.‡ Some speculated this meant Downing Street had expected Trump to win.§

Two weeks after the election Dominic Cummings quit. His destructive approach had echoed Trump's mayhem, bombast, disregard for rules and hatred of institutions.

---

* 'Pompeo says "there will be a smooth transition to our second Trump administration", despite Biden win', *Sky News*, 11 November 2020, https://news.sky.com/story/pompeo-says-there-will-be-a-smooth-transition-to-our-second-trump-administration-despite-biden-win-12129476.

† Patrick Wintour, 'Johnson urged to denounce Trump's claims of US election fraud', *The Guardian*, 5 November 2020, https://www.theguardian.com/politics/2020/nov/05/johnson-urged-to-denounce-trumps-unsubstantiated-us-election-claims.

‡ Alex Hern, 'Johnson's Biden win tweet contains hidden Trump congratulations', *The Guardian*, 10 November 2020, https://www.theguardian.com/politics/2020/nov/10/johnsons-biden-win-tweet-contains-hidden-trump-congratulations.

§ Chris Baynes, 'Boris Johnson's message congratulations Joe Biden on election victory contains hidden reference to Trump', *Independent*, 10 November 2020, https://www.independent.co.uk/news/uk/politics/boris-johnson-joe-biden-twitter-trump-b1720361.html.

Johnson's hostility to due process and integrity in government, however, was unabated. On 19 November an investigation found Home Secretary Priti Patel guilty of bullying civil servants.* This placed her in breach of the Ministerial Code, signed off by Johnson himself, which read: 'Harassing, bullying or other inappropriate or discriminating behaviour wherever it takes place is not consistent with the Ministerial Code and will not be tolerated.'† Johnson strongly defended her.

On 16 November the Johnson government announced that the death toll from Covid-19 stood at 52,147. The real figure was around 75,000.‡

With Trump gone, Johnson became the only leader of a Western liberal democracy openly set on challenging international norms. The former British ambassador to the US, Kim Darroch (who Johnson had sacked on Trump's insistence), remarked how 'fascinated' Johnson had seemed by Trump and his use of language: 'The limited vocabulary, the simplicity of the messaging, the disdain for political

---

* Jamie Grierson, 'Priti Patel bulling inquiry: why was it held and what did it find?, *The Guardian*, 20 November 2020, https://www.theguardian.com/politics/2020/nov/20/priti-patel-bullying-inquiry-why-was-it-held-and-what-did-it-find.

† Ministerial Code, https://assets.publishing.service.gov.uk/government/uploads/system/uploads/attachment_\data/file/826920/August-2019-MINISTERIAL-CODE-FINAL-FORMATTED-2.pdf.

‡ Chris Giles (@ChrisGiles_), 'We should recognize that Covid-19 is linked to around 75,000 UK deaths . . .', 17 November 2020, https://twitter.com/ChrisGiles_/status/1328683729263452166.

correctness, the sometimes incendiary imagery, and the at best intermittent relationship with facts and the truth.'

For Trump read Johnson. For Johnson read Trump. Trump's assault on truth has been beaten back (for the time being) in the United States. In Boris Johnson's Britain the culture of political lying and cheating grows deeper and more pervasive. Ordinary decency is ignored and the rule of law under attack. It's time to fight back.

Peter Oborne, 14 December 2020

Acknowledgements

I thank my researcher and collaborator Jan-Peter Westad for spending hours writing, researching, fact checking and keeping me cheerful. Richard Heller cast his eye over the manuscript and made many helpful suggestions. Will Moy and the staff at Full Fact taught me a great deal. In particular, I am grateful to Claire Milne.

I am indebted to Paul Seaward, director of the History of Parliament Trust, for giving me expert guidance on the history of lying in parliament and early political journalism. Dr Seaward reminded me that there is nothing new under the sun and the Popish Plot remains 'the mother of all English political lies'.

Tom Roberts gave instruction about Donald Trump, and also Rupert Murdoch. Annette Dittert, ARD's London bureau chief, helped me understand differing attitudes to public integrity in Britain and Germany. She also made penetrating comments on the manuscript. Thanks also to Mahdi Mustafa and Millie Cooke for further research.

Early ideas and facts for this book originally appeared on my website boris-johnson-lies.com. I thank everyone involved: Richard Assheton, Adam Bychawski, Tom Chivers, Charlie Peters, Michael Prodger, Dai Richards, William Wickstead and Aidan Dunlop.

Thanks also to Open Democracy, which published my long piece on how substantial sections of the British political press have allowed themselves to become the public manifestation of Boris Johnson's political machine when nobody else would.

I would like to thank Ian Marshall and Frances Jessop at Simon & Schuster, as well as Jonathan Wadman and Clare Hubbard, for their courtesy and their professionalism. They were a pleasure to deal with, as was my agent, Andrew Gordon.

And thanks to David Hearst, Editor-in-Chief at *Middle East Eye*, who allowed me to explore some of the ideas in this book in my weekly column, as well as giving me time off to write. Lindsay Codsi managed correspondence and kept me on the rails. Above all I thank my wife, Martine, for her patience and understanding.

Index